THE DEVELOPMENT OF WESTERN CIVILIZATION

*Narrative Essays in the History of Our Tradition from
Its Origins in Ancient Israel and Greece to the Present*

EDITED BY EDWARD W. FOX

THE DECLINE OF ROME

and the Rise of Mediaeval Europe

BY SOLOMON KATZ

The Decline of

ROME

and the Rise of

Mediaeval Europe

SOLOMON KATZ

UNIVERSITY OF WASHINGTON

Cornell University Press

ITHACA, NEW YORK

Foreword

THE proposition that each generation must rewrite history is more widely quoted than practiced. In the field of college texts on western civilization, the conventional accounts have been revised, and sources and supplementary materials have been developed; but it is too long a time since the basic narrative has been rewritten to meet the rapidly changing needs of new college generations. In the mid-twentieth century such an account must be brief, well written, and based on unquestioned scholarship and must assume almost no previous historical knowledge on the part of the reader. It must provide a coherent analysis of the development of western civilization and its basic values. It must, in short, constitute a systematic introduction to the collective memory of that tradition which we are being asked to defend. This series of narrative essays was undertaken in an effort to provide such a text for an introductory history survey course and is being published in the present form in the belief that the requirements of that one course reflected a need that is coming to be widely recognized.

Now that the classic languages, the Bible, the great historical novels, even most non-American history, have dropped out of the normal college preparatory program, it is imperative that a text in the history of European civilization be fully self-explanatory. This means not only that it must begin at the beginning, with the origins of our civilization in ancient Israel and Greece, but that it must introduce every name or event that takes an integral place in the account and ruthlessly delete all others no matter how firmly imbedded in historical protocol. Only thus simplified and complete will the narrative present a sufficiently clear outline of those major trends and developments that have led from the beginning of our recorded time to the most pressing of our current problems. This simplification, however, need not involve intellectual dilution or evasion. On the contrary, it can effectively raise rather than lower the level of presentation. It is on this assumption that the present series has been based, and each contributor has been urged to write for a mature and literate audience. It is hoped, therefore, that the essays may also prove profitable and rewarding to readers outside the college classroom.

The plan of the first part of the series is to sketch, in related essays, the narrative of our history from its origins to the eve of the French Revolution; each is to be written by a recognized scholar and is designed to serve as the basic reading for one week in a semester course. The developments of the nineteenth and twentieth centuries will be covered in a succeeding series which will provide the same quantity of reading material for each week of the second semester. This scale of presentation has been adopted in the conviction that any understanding of the central problem of the preservation of the integrity and dignity of the individual human being depends first on an examination of the origins of our tradition in the politics and philosophy of the ancient Greeks and the religion of the ancient Hebrews and then on a relatively more detailed knowledge of its recent development within our industrial urban society.

The decision to devote equal space to twenty-five centuries and to a century and a half was based on analogy with the human memory. Those events most remote tend to be remembered in least detail but often with a sense of clarity and perspective that is absent in more recent and more crowded recollections. If the roots of our tradition must be identified, their relation to the present must be carefully developed. The nearer the narrative approaches contemporary times, the more difficult and complicated this becomes. Recent experience must be worked over more carefully and in more detail if it is to contribute effectively to an understanding of the contemporary world.

It may be objected that the series attempts too much. The attempt is being made, however, on the assumption that any historical development should be susceptible of meaningful treatment on any scale and in the realization that a very large proportion of today's college students do not have more time to invest in this part of their education. The practical alternative appears to lie between some attempt to create a new brief account of the history of our tradition and the abandonment of any serious effort to communicate the essence of that tradition to all but a handful of our students. It is the conviction of everyone contributing to this series that the second alternative must not be accepted by default.

In a series covering such a vast sweep of time, few scholars would find themselves thoroughly at home in the fields covered by more than one or two of the essays. This means, in practice, that almost every essay should be written by a different author. In spite of apparent drawbacks, this procedure promises real advantages. Each contributor will be in a position to set higher standards of accuracy and insight in an essay encompassing a major portion of the field of his life's work than could ordinarily be expected in surveys of some ten or twenty centuries. The inevitable discontinuity of style and interpretation could be modified by editorial coordination; but it was felt that some discontinuity was in itself desirable. No illusion is more easily acquired by the student in an elementary course, or is more prejudicial to the efficacy of such a course, than that a single smoothly articulated text represents the very substance of history itself. If the shift from author to author, week by week, raises difficulties for the beginning student, they are difficulties that will not so much impede his progress as contribute to his growth.

In this essay, *The Decline of Rome and the Rise of Mediaeval Europe*, Mr. Solomon Katz presents a brief narrative account of the most awe-inspiring tragedy of western Europe: the failure of civilized men to maintain the most civilized society the world had yet known. From the time of Augustine to that of Gibbon, Europe lived under the shadow of the Roman catastrophe, and hardly had our ancestors emerged from this shade onto the sunny slope of the century of progress when dark prophets began to read the destiny of modern civilization in the decline of ancient Rome. Historical observers have found it all but impossible to contemplate this glacial cataclysm without drawing moral conclusions, discovering religious revelations, or describing scientific verities, thereby endowing the field with as much significance for western philosophy of history as for the history of the West. Confronted with this double tradition, Mr. Katz chose first to focus his essay clearly on the central narrative of the period and then succeeded in interweaving deft evaluations of critical points of major interpretations of the history that will at once capture the imagination of beginners and command the respect of scholars.

Both author and editor wish to express their gratitude to Mr. M. L. W. Laistner and Mr. Paul P. Cram for many helpful suggestions.

EDWARD WHITING FOX

Ithaca, New York
November, 1954

Contents

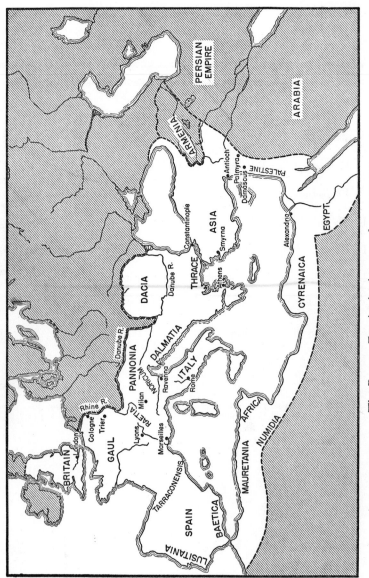

The Roman Empire in the second century A.D.

Prologue

ROME, once a tiny village on the Tiber River in Italy, emerged as ruler of the western world. It had begun (tradition says in 753 B.C.) as a community of farmers, and its early history does not seem to have differed in essentials from that of any other Mediterranean city-state which, early in its career, sent its kings packing. To replace the monarchy, these farmer folk, by peaceful evolution and by revolution and civil war, formed an aristocratic republic controlled by a senate and a senatorial nobility. Under this constitution they brought Italy within their sway and began to master the Mediterranean world. Meantime they learned the ways of commerce and industry, and their simple culture was modified, its content made richer and more sophisticated, by contact with the older and more advanced civilizations of Greece and the Orient. This apprenticeship prepared the Romans to carry on the traditions which the Greeks and Hebrews had brilliantly established and so to complete the foundations of Europe and of the civilization of the West.

The burden of conquest and of governing the empire that conquest brought into existence proved too much for the essentially amateur and civilian institutions of the senatorial republic, and the ancestral constitutional government of Rome seemed about to end in military despotism or to dissolve in anarchy when it was replaced by the rule of one man. This was the work of Caius Julius Caesar (assassinated, 44 B.C.) and of his grandnephew and heir, Caius Julius Caesar Octavianus (63 B.C.–A.D. 14), whom we know best by the name Augustus. Originally this word meant little more than "honored," with the added suggestion of "revered," and this meaning gives a clue to the foundation on which the new regime rested: it was gratitude and admiration for the man who had restored order and saved the state. If gratitude soon made him seem a little more than mortal and a little less than divine, and if he was honored in death as a divine being, this was consistent with the attitude of the ancient world toward hero-saviors, and not surprising in the circumstances.

It would be a mistake to conclude that this shift away from a republic in theory to an empire in practice marks an abrupt or complete rupture with tradition. History knows few if any such breaks in the life of states and civilizations, and Augustus was careful to keep the ancestral frame of tradition intact. He kept the keys and title deeds to power carefully in his own hands and excluded the Senate and the senatorial aristocracy from access to them, yet he did not liquidate the aristocracy and it retained important duties and remained a major element of continuity throughout much of the long history of the Empire. In this Augustus was, perhaps, following a program of conciliation and conservative reform initiated before the collapse of the old government. In any event, his policy in these matters fixed the character and, broadly speaking, determined the future of the new constitution.

Had he chosen to do so, Augustus might have ruled as *"imperator"* (our word, "emperor"), the title by which the army knew him as commander-in-chief. In that case he would have founded a military despotism. Or he could have built his regime around the title *"dominus,"* which carries the implication of lordship, even ownership, of the Empire and its people. Such a domination would have instituted a civilian despotism. He did neither, and the key to his policy is the word *"princeps"* (our word, "prince"). This means "first," with the notion of first in achievement and so in honor. The title had a republican tradition behind it, yet it was as *princeps,* that is, "first citizen," that Augustus elected to rule the world. This fitted the strictly legal aspects of his position, for in law he was never more than a simple citizen clothed by the Senate with an authority that was ultimately derived from the Roman people, just as it supposedly had been in the early days of the city-state republic. From the word *"princeps"* comes the term "Principate," often used to designate the government of the Roman Empire. And it is a proper term despite the fact that after the second century of the Christian era the government was seldom anything but a naked military despotism, because every emperor who ever wore the purple, whatever his public acts or claims, remained in law a citizen whose authority ultimately derived from the people. For this reason the Principate has been aptly described as a "disguised constitutional monarchy."

If, at first glance, the point seems far-fetched, it must be remembered that had this disguised constitutional monarchy not been embedded in Roman law and later in Christian thinking, the traditions bequeathed by Rome to the West might well have been those of a military rather than a civilian state, of a lawless despotism instead of a government of laws. Under such conditions it is extremely unlikely that free societies, including our own, could have come into existence in modern western civilization. And had they by some miracle emerged, they would have found it difficult if not impossible to endure.

This suggests that in the long life of societies and civilizations it is not necessarily the most striking and dramatic elements that are the most potent and lasting. For this reason the words in which Professor Rostovtzeff sums up the Roman contribution to modern civilization make an admirable introduction to any study of the Roman Empire:

The ancient world slowly grew old and decrepit and was reduced to dust; but a new life grew up upon the ruins, and the new edifice of European civilization was built on a foundation that had remained firm and sound. The new building rose stone by stone, but its main lines were determined by the old substructure, and many of the old stones were used for further service. Though that world grew old, it never died and never disappeared; it lives on in us, as the groundwork of our thought, our attitude to religion, our art, our social and political institutions, and even our material civilization.[1]

Any twentieth-century estimate of the situation and future prospects of western free societies which aims at realism and accuracy must take some account of the cause and course of events that took place in the Roman Empire the better part of two millennia ago.

[1] M. Rostovtzeff, *A History of the Ancient World*, II (Oxford, 1928), 359.

CHAPTER I

Prelude to Crisis

THE Principate, by re-establishing order and healing the deep wounds of social and civil war, restored unity to the Roman world for two centuries and, by creating a new efficient machinery of government, gave the Mediterranean lands security and prosperity such as they had never known before and civilization has seldom seen since. The climax of this accomplishment was reached in the second century of the Christian era, a period known as the Age of the Antonines (138–192), and particularly under the two greatest Antonine emperors, Antoninus Pius and his successor Marcus Aurelius Antoninus, the philosopher-emperor, who had to spend the last years of his life at the head of his armies defending the frontier against the Germans. This is the time which Edward Gibbon in *The Decline and Fall of the Roman Empire* regarded as the happiest age mankind has known. His book came out in 1776, and Gibbon, thanks to his massive scholarship and majestic prose, has kept a place among the greatest writers of history ever since. In the opening chapters of this magnificent work Gibbon describes how, in the Age of the Antonines, citizen and provincial, freeman and slave, rich and poor, from the Atlantic Ocean to the Euphrates River, from the Rhine and the Danube to the Sahara Desert, were united under "the immense majesty of the Roman peace." It is certain that the efficiency, enlightenment, and cosmopolitanism that lay behind this achievement are the most striking aspects of the second century. That they were also the most significant is, perhaps, another matter.

Gibbon's words read almost like a paraphrase of the thought of Virgil (who died in 19 B.C.) in the sixth book of the *Aeneid*, when he proclaimed the ideal of the Principate of Augustus:

> But thou, O Roman, learn with sovereign sway
> To rule the nations. Thy great art shall be
> To keep the world in lasting peace, to spare
> The humbled foe and crush to earth the proud.[1]

In the Fourth Eclogue he prophesied an "age foretold" when

> The vast world-process brings a new-born time.
> Once more the Virgin comes and Saturn's reign,
> Behold a heaven-born offspring earthward hies! [2]

This era, he goes on to say, would "free the world from perpetual fear" under the "reign of a golden people." Christian enthusiasm saw in these words a prophecy of the birth of Christ. It was, rather, a vision of an imperial golden age, perhaps with a veiled reference to a child of the imperial house. In the next century the same belief in the mission of Rome was voiced by Pliny the Elder (who died a martyr to his scientific interests in the famous eruption of Vesuvius which wiped out Pompeii in A.D. 79). "Italy," he wrote,

[1] *The Aeneid of Virgil,* tr. by T. C. Williams (New York, 1908), p. 218.

[2] *The Georgics and Eclogues of Virgil,* tr. by T. C. Williams (Cambridge, Mass., 1915), p. 138.

"has been selected by the gods in order to unite scattered empires, to soften customs and unite by the community of one language the diverse and barbarous dialects of so many nations, to bestow on men the intercourse of ideas and humanity, in a word—that all the peoples of the world should have one fatherland." [3]

The Age of the Antonines

Under the Antonines these visions were in almost literal truth fulfilled. Secure behind natural frontiers of ocean, rivers, and desert, behind the *limes* (an artificial frontier of fortified military encampments that linked the Rhine and the Danube), and behind the walls that kept distant Britain safe, the Roman Empire in the second century seemed to lie impregnable. It was "one world" of more than a million and a quarter square miles at its greatest extent, where dwelt between fifty or sixty millions of people: Italians, Greeks, Illyrians, Egyptians, Celts, Germans, and a host of others.

To Tertullian, one of the Fathers of the Latin Church, this pagan empire, at the end of the second century, was

a world every day better known, better cultivated, and more civilized than before. Everywhere roads are traced, every district is known, every country opened to commerce. Smiling fields have invaded the forests; flocks and herds have routed the wild beasts; the very sands are sown; the rocks are planted; the marshes drained. There are now as many cities as there were once solitary cottages. Reefs and shoals have lost their terrors. Wherever there is a trace of life there are houses and human habitations, well-ordered governments and civilized life. [4]

[3] Pliny, *Natural History*, III, V, 39–40 (author's translation).
[4] Tertullian, *Concerning the Soul*, ch. 30 (author's translation).

Other Greek and Roman writers, law codes, archaeological
finds, coins, papyri, and thousands of inscriptions from all
parts of the Empire support this Christian estimate.

The road system to which Tertullian refers owed its
beginning to the Republic, for as Rome expanded her sway
her roads stretched out over the world. The main highways
were laid out originally for military and administrative
purposes: to facilitate the rapid movement of troops from
one part of the Empire to another and to link Rome more
effectively with her provinces. The city itself became the
focus of world communications, the center of a net of trunk
highways, adequately maintained and patrolled and supplemented by local roads. The sea lanes, kept clear of pirates,
lighted in places by beacons, and sometimes marked for
navigation, led, like the roads, to Italy and Rome. Thanks
to this system, the cities and hamlets, the mines and quar-
ries, of the civilized world were linked as never before.
Men—Roman soldiers, Roman lawyer-administrators, merchants, students, artists, scholars of every land; goods—
domestic and foreign; and ideas—not native only, but alien
too—moved with a freedom and speed not again approached
in the same vast region until the coming of the railroad in
the nineteenth century. Fresh life and prosperity came to
ancient cities, new cities sprang into sudden being, and in
them a cosmopolitan, universal civilization began to take
final shape.

The earliest home of this new civilization was Greece
and the city-states of the Hellenized East. As the Empire
expanded, similar cities grew up in the West, the advance
posts of the civilization the Principate was rapidly making
universal. On the shores of the Mediterranean Sea, the Black
Sea, and the Red Sea were thriving, cosmopolitan, com-

mercial centers: Tarragona, Narbonne, Marseilles, Carthage, Brindisi, Ostia, Corinth, Alexandria, Smyrna, Ephesus; along the rivers lay Bordeaux, Lyons, Trier, Cologne; along the roads Damascus, Tarsus, Antioch. In Britain and along the Rhine and the Danube towns grew out of military stations or alongside them as merchants gathered to supply the needs of the soldiers and as veterans received grants of land in the areas in which they had served, and settled there. Such were the cities of Bonn, Mainz, Strasbourg, and Wiesbaden on the Rhine; Vienna, Budapest, and Belgrade on the Danube; York and Gloucester in Britain. Rome, the largest city of the Empire, had over a million inhabitants, and there were at least half a dozen other large cities, each with a population of a quarter of a million or more. Most of the cities of the Empire, however, and especially those in the West, were small towns by our standards, since the population of Europe then was far less dense than it is today.

In the zone of military occupation across the Rhine, 160 towns are known; across the Danube in Dacia (modern Roumania) some 120 cities can be named. In other provinces the record is similar—everywhere cities grew up, at once the foundation and impressive evidence of the life and civilization the Roman Empire was creating and sustaining. And everywhere the cities and the rural districts that fed them were like small replicas of the capital itself. Whether in Britain, along the Rhine or Danube, the Rhone or Moselle, in Africa, Asia, or Syria, on the fringes of the desert, or on the coast, a traveler from Rome might feel at home amid familiar temples, fora, baths, triumphal arches, theaters, and amphitheaters. New cities and new sections of older cities were laid out according to well-conceived plans; long and sometimes colonnaded streets radiated from a central square.

Towns, new or old, had adequate supplies of water provided by aqueducts, good drainage facilities, well-paved and sometimes lighted streets and public squares, impressive public buildings and private homes, many of which were equipped with such amenities as mosaic floors, glass windows, running water, and heating systems.

The Roman Peace

The *Pax Romana* which made this life possible was protected by an army of some 400,000 men. This force, microscopic for the region to be guarded, was highly trained, superbly disciplined in the greatest days of the Empire, and remarkably mobile considering the state of communications in the world of the time. Never since then has the same area enjoyed so much security at so little cost in manpower, man hours, and money. On the northern frontiers there were occasional border skirmishes, but no serious threat to Roman security; in the East the Parthians were no longer formidable enough to present a major challenge to Roman authority. The troops themselves, whether legionaries or auxiliaries, filled with a fine *esprit de corps*, a pride in their traditions, and a consciousness of their mission as soldiers of Rome, were active agents of Romanization in the areas in which they were stationed. When they had completed twenty-five years of military service, the auxiliaries were granted Roman citizenship, and they settled usually in the provinces in which they had served. Hence there was in the frontier areas a steady addition of Roman citizens, men who had learned in the army something of the meaning of Rome, while the provinces from which these men were recruited felt that they too had a stake in Rome. As settlements of veterans, merchants, and others developed into towns, natives and Romans met and mingled in the frontier zones, and Roman culture sifted down slowly but surely and began to leaven the barbarian mass and to prepare the slow formation of future nationalities.

Roman administration was stable, efficient, and generally honest. The government was managed by experts in a close-knit civil service under the control of the emperor. Citizenship, no less highly valued now than before, was bestowed more generously upon deserving provincials. The governing class, indeed emperors themselves, had ceased to be a narrow group of Italians and was recruited increasingly from the upper class of the provincial cities. The Roman government tolerated local customs and traditions, made no effort to impose uniformity of culture, and insisted on one thing only from the countless minority groups under its rule: they must keep the Roman peace. Nevertheless, distinctions and barriers between Rome and the provinces tended to diminish, sometimes to the vanishing point. Although all the municipalities were under the ultimate control of the emperor, varying degrees of self-government were accorded to them. In the midst of this bewildering administrative diversity the common institutions of the Empire were potent bonds of community—the army, the courts, the great administrative system, were all powerful, if informal instruments of education. The army fulfilled a tremendous function, far greater than is easy to imagine unless we analyze in detail the character of its organization. Above all, there was the person of the emperor, the symbol and agent of imperial unity.

The Social Structure

Social classes, it is true, continued well defined, yet they were also more fluid than in republican days or at the beginning of the Principate, and movement from one class to another was more easily accomplished. Below the emperor stood the Senate, still the chief governing class, although its powers and prerogatives now depended upon the good will of the sovereign. Its ranks were steadily replenished from wealthy equestrians and members of the municipal aristocracy of Italy and the provinces.

The equestrian order derived its place and power from the fact that the emperors relied on its members as a balance, particularly for the senatorial order. Recruited from the lower ranks of society—lesser army officers, municipal aristocrats, freedmen of prominence and others who had shown enterprise and ability—they were employed increasingly for the more important imperial posts, and in contrast to those of the senatorial order, which had an ancient grudge against the Principate, they were more wholehearted in their loyalty. In the cities of Italy and of the provinces there was still in the second century an influential governing class, large landowners and prosperous businessmen who could afford the heavy donations and outlays in behalf of their cities which ancient custom imposed as part of the responsibilities of leading men in the Graeco-Roman world.

Below the upper classes of tradition, wealth, and office, and providing new blood for them in the dynamic society of the Principate, were small business people, clerks from public and private employ who had a head for figures and could read, and sometimes even artisans. This general fluidity—one of the greatest contributions of Rome to western civilization—had a good deal to do with the efficiency and endurance of the Empire and with the loyalty of the provinces in times of crisis and disaster.

In the lowest strata of society a quite different situation existed. Everywhere in the country districts there was a mass made up of small tenant-farmers, hired hands, and slaves, who were barely touched by the urban civilization that was characteristic of Graeco-Roman development. They had counterparts in the cities, folk who had the least possible share in the enormous intellectual, social, and financial profits of the new civilization. These were free wage earners, artisans, unskilled laborers, and slaves. In city and country alike this mass teetered precariously between survival and extinction. Sudden disaster—a poor harvest, flood, fire, inflation, an epidemic—could tip the balance to ruin. A prolonged crisis, long war, civil or foreign, or a series of disasters in close succession would tip it to extinction for large sections of them.

Such a threat was not peculiar to Italy, to the Empire, or to antiquity. It stalked the ancient world as it stalks the modern, perhaps never more menacingly than today. The Romans who had inherited and enlarged the Greek humane tradition reacted to such disasters in the same way that we, who are also heirs to the same tradition, respond to them: they fed the starving. This gave rise in time to the formula of a satirist: "Bread and circuses." There is not the least doubt that this was a monument of futility as a solution; it bred a social cancer and became a terrible drain on the budget. But the alternative, the desperate rioting of the starving, would have cost still more in social erosion.

The Economic Foundations

Thanks to the Roman peace, the Empire attained its highest economic development. Industry and commerce flourished, especially in the East, where the cities with a longer tradition of trade and manufacturing were situated; but the West, more important as a source of raw materials, made its own contribution to Rome's wealth. From the West came the bulk of Rome's metal ores: tin, lead, silver, and gold from Spain; tin from Britain; gold and silver from Dacia (Roumania); iron from Noricum (roughly Austria and part of Bavaria). The western provinces produced a surplus of agricultural products which were shipped to Rome and to other parts of the Empire. By this time parts of the West began to develop simple industries and the commerce that went with them. Gaul in particular manufactured native pottery, the *terra sigillata*, a red-glazed ware, which soon outsold in local markets the Italian Samian or Arretine ware which it imitated, and finally competed successfully with its prototype in Italian and other markets. Gaul, and somewhat later Britain, had important manufactures of glass and bronze-ware, Spain produced swords and armor, Gaul was famous for its textiles. The eastern provinces furnished some valuable raw materials, marble and other stones, timber, fish, as well as farm products, but the East was a more notable source of fine manufactured goods: glassware, metalware, and textiles from Egypt and Syria, woolens from Asia Minor, luxury goods of one kind or another from various places. In all this industrial output, eastern or western, the small workshop—in which a craftsman was assisted perhaps by a few slaves—was the characteristic unit of production. Even where larger "factories" were to be found, as for example in the manufacture of Samian ware in Italy or Gaul or in the building-materials industries—the production of bricks, tiles, or lead water pipes—the number of slaves or free workers was, by our standards, very small, generally fewer than twenty-five, almost never over a hundred.

There was a lively interprovincial trade in the necessities

of life, such as wheat, oil, and wine, as well as in the cheaper textiles and pottery and metal utensils of daily use which needed regular replacement. The army was one of the best customers in the Empire. Not only did it provide a market for farm products and manufactured goods brought from near and far, but it also fostered the economic development of the frontier regions, as merchants gathered around the military camps and stations to cater to the needs of the troops. As the Empire prospered and the demand for luxuries increased, there was an expanding trade in luxury goods, especially from the eastern provinces and from beyond the frontiers. Provincial and Italian businessmen traveled across the borders through the barbarian lands to the north as far as Scandinavia, or through Parthia to the east, or southward down the Red Sea and across the Indian Ocean. A uniform and dependable imperial coinage facilitated this active trade and served as another symbol of Rome's might and majesty. So, too, the standardization of language—Latin throughout the Empire but especially in the West, and Greek in the East—promoted trade and fostered unity. Nevertheless, while there was economic as well as political unity, there was apparent a tendency toward economic decentralization and self-sufficiency, as provincials began to produce goods which they had once imported from Italy or from other provinces. The centrifugal forces were not yet strong enough to tear the Empire asunder, but already in the second century they were gaining momentum.

The Agricultural Classes

Although the Roman Empire was highly urbanized and enjoyed an active trade and industry, the vast majority of the people, provincials and Italians alike, then and until very recent times, gained their living from agriculture, either directly by tilling the soil or indirectly from the ownership of farmland. The chief food crops were wheat, olives, and wines produced for local distribution and consumption in near-by cities or for export to feed the huge population of the capital as well as for the army on the frontiers. Some farms raised flax for linen, others were essentially ranches producing meat, wool, and hides for local use or interprovincial trade.

This rural population, like country folk everywhere and in all times, was pretty well cut off from the movement of ideas and clung to the past, the old ways and the ancestral attitudes. They responded less readily to Romanization than city folk, and this had important effects on their position in later times, as the history of the Later Empire and the Middle Ages shows clearly. A minor but suggestive illustration of this is the change in the sense of the Latin ancestor of our word "pagan." Originally it meant a countryman, a rustic, a peasant. Because the rural class clung longest to the old religion, the Latin word for countryman, when Christianity advanced, came to mean "heathen," as does the English word "pagan" which is derived from it.

We do not know as much about these rural people under the Empire as we should like to, but there are signs that they did not share equally with the upper and middle classes of the cities in the material advantages of Roman rule. The number of independent small landowners declined steadily as more and more farmers became tenants of absentee landlords on the estates held by the emperor, by the imperial aristocracy, by wealthy provincials who belonged to the municipal aristocracy, or by temples.

Our data are not complete enough for positive, sweeping

generalizations, but some notion of the size of the normal small farm in republican times can be gained from the Gracchan land-reform law of 133 B.C. This appears to have divided public lands into farmsteads of about twenty acres, which were given to the poor. In imperial times some estates were as small as 130 acres, others ran to 1,000 acres. Those of the emperors, swollen by gift, bequest, and confiscation, were vastly larger. Under the Republic, in the days of easy conquests and an abundant supply of captives, the use of slaves had increased greatly. In addition, a good deal of land once used for cereal production had been turned to grazing. Both developments had a bad effect on the small freeholder, who was thus brought to face strong competition from slave labor on large estates. Under the Empire the character of war changed into frontier guardianship and the sources of cheap slaves dried up. Nevertheless, large estates continued to operate and even increase in number and size, although *coloni*, that is, free tenant farmers, according to the original use of the word, began to replace slave labor on them. Some *coloni* kept their original free status; others were among the ancestors of the mediaeval serf. The tendency toward self-sufficiency already noticed in connection with provincial trade and industry began to appear on these larger estates; many of them were producing an ever greater proportion of manufactured goods for their own use or even for sale in near-by cities. Each of these changes is apparent in the second century, and in these respects the mediaeval manor was already casting its shadow before.

The Cultural Outlook

The period of the Antonines, with the efficient and even beneficent imperial government, the years unbroken by difficulties, and the relatively high standard of general prosperity might well have been expected to produce a brilliant culture. Spiritual vigor and creativeness, however, did not go hand in hand with unity, peace, power, and prosperity, and the general poverty of intellectual life was a portent of decline or at least of stagnation. Art, to be sure, showed new vitality in medal engraving and portrait sculpture, but on the whole art and literature became conventional and dull. Imitation and pedantic affectation largely took the place of originality. For the cultivated and leisure class, from which the writers came, the freshness and savor of life were somehow wanting. Confidence in the possibilities of this world seemed to be waning, and the writers of the period sought flight from reality by producing a literature which had little connection with the life of the times. Since the present age seemed dull and uncreative, the leading authors wrote on themes that were irrelevant to life in a style that was neither fresh nor spontaneous, but a nostalgic attempt to recapture the flavor of an earlier and a happier age.

It was, however, not only the writers of the Antonine period who seem to have found little to attract them in the contemporary world. In general there was a sense of insecurity, a brooding quest for hope and salvation after death. Intellectuals turned to the consolations of philosophical schools in which reason and clear thinking often yielded to emotionalism, mysticism, and superstition. The mass of the people were finding a substitute for a world which was too much for them in the Oriental mystery religions. These cults, which had been coming into the Mediterranean world for centuries, will be dealt with in more detail later. Here it is enough to point out that they were bound up with the sufferings of hero-saviors, that they offered purification to the individual in this life and also held out a priceless hope of personal immortality. Among the religions which came out of the East, Christianity, a late arrival, was destined to triumph only after a vigorous contest. As men were increasingly beset by troubles, as hope for improvement waned, these religions exerted a tremendous mass appeal. More and more men sought courage and escape in other-worldly mystery religions.

Symptoms of Decline

What was wrong? Even before the crisis of the third century, even before the margin of security was reduced during the Principate of Marcus Aurelius (161–180), there were factors which stifled initiative and killed enterprise. The tranquillity of the Antonine Age was deceptive; peace existed but precariously, prosperity was neither widespread nor deeply rooted. The seeds of decay were germinating beneath the surface and soon sprouted under the favoring circumstances of foreign war and internal chaos.

Long ago Rome had granted or acknowledged the freedom of cities, especially in the East, to manage local affairs through their own senates and municipal magistrates, their own financial systems, and their own courts. The imperial government had always retained the right to exercise an overriding control, but in general it did not infringe upon the wide sphere of local self-government. This generous privilege had encouraged a loyalty to Rome and a pride in the Empire as well as a civic pride which at least in the governing class of the municipalities had served as a powerful psychological stimulus to mental and material achievement.

The Decline of the Cities

Despite their apparently flourishing condition, the cities of the Empire, focal points of ancient civilization, were showing symptoms of economic decline and their inhabitants were displaying signs of a loss of civic initiative. Membership in the Empire was still highly prized, but Romans and non-Romans alike were yielding their municipal liberties to a paternalistic and increasingly autocratic central government which more and more bent men to its will. Regulation had not yet become regimentation, but the imperial administration was holding the control reins more tightly and more often than before was drawing upon them.

The Fiscal Crisis

The long wars of Marcus Aurelius and the devastating plague which accompanied them gave an additional impetus to a decline which had set in earlier. Local and imperial taxes mounted, towns overspent their resources on civic improvements, and a bureaucratic central government required more funds for the amenities of peace and the necessities of war. Wars had once enabled Rome to balance the budget by adding new areas for exploitation and by bringing in vast sums as booty. The Roman economy had expanded with the Empire. Now, as wars were mainly defensive and as the frontiers remained fixed, the economy itself became static or even contracted. The imperial government found itself hard pressed to raise the funds required to maintain an army of soldiers and civil servants. Since excessive financial demands were made upon the municipalities and the local officeholders, many of these men sought escape from what had once been an honor but was now a costly burden. The aversion to municipal office was not yet widespread, but the signs were ominous and foreshadowed the breakdown of the system of local government.

It is one of the ironies of history that the decline was sharply intensified during the Principate of Marcus Aurelius, the very type of philosopher-king whom Plato had regarded as the ideal ruler. A period of incessant wars on the strategic northern and eastern frontiers succeeded peace. Soon after his accession, the northern defense line was stripped of large detachments of troops for service in the Parthian Wars in the East. Barbarian tribes, especially the Marcomanni and Quadi living beyond the Upper Rhine and Danube, overwhelmed the weakened garrisons in 167, breached the northern frontiers, swarmed into the border provinces, and invaded northern Italy itself. Only with difficulty was their advance halted, and only after long years of heavy fighting were they defeated in the Marcomannic Wars. The first great invasion from the north was finally repelled, but the threat of wandering barbarians (as the Romans called their Germanic neighbors to the north) continued to hang over the Empire.

The emperor's troubles multiplied as an epidemic brought back by the troops returning from the Parthian Wars spread like wildfire through the western provinces and caused thousands of deaths. Famine was widespread as farmers died of plague or deserted their fields in the face of enemy advance, and a weakening economy was further depressed. Meanwhile the expenses of the state mounted. The prolonged series of campaigns was costly, the bureaucracy was expanding rapidly, extravagance in imperial court circles was great. The financial structure of the Empire was essentially unsound. In peacetime there were generally ample revenues, but in time of war there was no capital reserve nor was it possible to create a national debt in order to meet the extraordinary expenses. The auctioning of the crown jewels in order to procure money for war was a desperate expedient to which Marcus was reduced. It was the provincials, the inhabitants of towns, who were called upon to bear heavier burdens, to undertake fresh liturgies or so-called voluntary services, either by furnishing additional sums in cash or by providing food, lodging, and transport for imperial troops.

Not until the third century were the full effects of this policy felt, but while Marcus Aurelius was still alive there were signs that the vitality and prosperity of the cities were being undermined. The middle and upper classes were being increasingly subjected to the overriding needs and interests of the central government. In its quest for money the government imposed heavier burdens than the towns could assume and thereby throttled enterprise. In its search for efficiency the imperial bureaucracy ultimately destroyed local self-government. Imperial commissioners, for example, were imposed upon cities whose financial condition was precarious. As early as Trajan's reign (98–117) such special administrative experts (called *correctores*, *curatores*, or *logistai*) had been appointed by the emperor to supervise and overhaul the disordered finances of cities and even whole provinces. Begun as an emergency measure to end financial mismanagement, imperial control over local administration tended to become a regular practice. Thus the action of the second-century emperors paved the way for the tighter control of local affairs by the central government in the following century. The process of civic decay had begun within the cities themselves, but the corrosive action of the state was rapidly wearing away municipal liberty, a keystone of the structure of Roman civilization.

For the common man, the farm worker, or the humbler folk in the cities of the Empire, the burden of life became harder. True, the condition of slaves had improved under the impact of a growing humanitarianism; true, with the drying up of the sources of slaves, slave labor was gradually being replaced by free labor, but the evil of slavery was not examined, let alone cured. The pauperization of the mass of free men advanced, and if slaves gained freedom, free men were reduced to the status of subjects—an equality of subjection to a state which was ever more autocratic. The causes of social conflict, repressed rather than excised, festered beneath the surface.

The Unsolved Problems of Empire

These are a few of the signs of decline which manifested themselves during the reign of Marcus Aurelius. In themselves they may not have been serious; given time, but more important, given thought, they might have been prevented from becoming aggravated. But no respite was granted and the crisis worsened as a decent, if improvident, emperor was succeeded by a worthless son. The Romans in general showed little interest in ideas, little perception of the theoretical bases of the state and its economy. Many problems, which perhaps only in retrospect and with the advantage we have of hindsight seem fundamental, were left untouched. So the cancer of slavery was not cured, the growing poverty of the urban population and the increasing misery of the rural folk were dealt with, if at all, by palliatives such as doles, subsidies, and benefactions. The prob-

lem of checking the growing parasitism of the cities upon
the countryside, the problem of reversing the trend toward
political centralization in order to keep pace with an advancing economic decentralization, the problem of establishing
representation for the provinces, the problem of preserving
municipal autonomy within the framework of a world state,
the problem of providing adequate revenues for the state
without destroying the taxpayers—these questions were not
considered, or, if they were, were not solved. As external
pressures from barbarians and Persians increased and as internal chaos mounted, some solution to these and other
problems would have to be found if the Empire were not to
disintegrate.

When Marcus Aurelius died in 180, the Empire still
seemed secure. Coins might still attest the "Eternity of the
Roman People." The Romans had created and preserved a
unified world, and they seemed strong enough to perpetuate
unity and security. They failed, and the signs of their
failure became clearer as the third century advanced. A
hundred years of crisis followed the death of Marcus
Aurelius. When the Empire recovered, its political, economic, social, and cultural structure was profoundly altered.

CHAPTER II

Crisis and Recovery

OUR history," wrote the contemporary historian Dio Cassius in describing the transition from the mild rule of Marcus Aurelius to the brutal despotism of those who succeeded him, "now descends from a kingdom of gold to one of iron and rust." [1] Closer study has shown that there was dross in the golden age of the Antonines and more precious materials in the iron age of the third century. Nevertheless, that century was one of crisis and chaos, depression and disorder, invasion and violence. It witnessed the triumph of military absolutism over the civilian constitution of the Principate established by Augustus and maintained with some changes by his successors. The integrity of the Empire was almost shattered by the internecine wars of rival aspirants for the throne, the incursions of barbarians from the north, and the attacks of the new Sassanian Empire from the East. Costly civil and foreign wars, the greed of the troops, and the mounting expenses of an expanding bureaucracy bled the state white. In its quest for security and solvency a desperate and relentless government, heedless of those rights which Rome had once granted her citizens and subjects, oppressed town and country. The stormy times in which men

[1] Dio Cassius, *Roman History*, LXXII, 36.4.

lived could not help but be reflected in their intellectual and spiritual interests.

The Military Basis of Imperial Authority

The power of the army to make and murder emperors, the control of the Roman world by generals elevated to the highest office in the Empire by their troops and in turn overthrown by them—this is the main thread running through the history of the third century. The Empire tottered precariously as the throne was seized by one short-lived ruler after another. Once the servants of the state, the soldiers were now its masters. As the need for them became greater because of the intensified pressure of enemies on the frontiers, the soldiers learned their power and were increasingly insubordinate. Only with difficulty did some of the emperors succeed in playing a larger role than that of puppets in the hands of an unruly army. Yet these emperors, whose portrait busts reveal their toughness and grim resolution, fought their way to the pinnacle of power with the support of the troops and then succeeded in mastering them and in arresting the disintegration of the Empire. From the Danubian provinces, Illyria, Thrace, the Orient, Africa, from the old Roman aristocracy, the new provincial aristocracy, the peasantry, above all from the army, came these emperors who ruled Rome and tried, each in his own way, to prevent her ruin. If it was the army which by its arbitrary exercise of usurped power almost brought Rome to her knees, it was also the army which, under the leadership of the soldier-emperors at the end of the century, enabled her to survive.

For nearly a hundred years before the death of Marcus Aurelius the emperors had tried to select their successors on the basis of merit and ability. But when Marcus reverted to the dynastic principle of succession in place of the "choice of the best," he paved the way for corruption and misrule which brought in their train civil war, bloodshed, and military despotism. The rule of Marcus' megalomaniac son, Commodus (180–192), was marked by palace intrigues and conspiracies and by unrest in the army and in the Praetorian Guard, which finally murdered the emperor. Once more, as on the death of Nero in 68, the secret was discovered that an emperor could be chosen elsewhere than at Rome. Now, as then, the Praetorian Guard took the lead in murdering and creating emperors. The armies stationed in the provinces then followed suit and offered their own candidates for the throne. Henceforth the army was the dominant factor in the selection of the emperors, and the Senate, which was in theory the constitutional source of the emperor's authority, was powerless to do more than confirm the will of the troops.

Repenting their choice of a new emperor within three months, the praetorians brought about his downfall and sold the vacant throne at auction to the highest bidder. But Septimius Severus, governor of Upper Pannonia, led the troops under his command on Rome and seized power (193–211). When he disposed of his rivals, the governors of Syria and Britain who had themselves been saluted as emperors by their troops, his office was secure. As long as he enjoyed the support of the army, he could scorn the Senate and treat it as another instrument of his autocratic rule.

The Severan Reforms

In the intervals between successful wars against his rivals

and against the Parthians on the eastern frontier, Septimius instituted a program of reform. Since he had gained the throne with the help of the army, he was afraid that he might be toppled from it by the same soldiers or by those under the command of generals no less ambitious than he had been. By subdividing large provinces and consequently reducing the number of troops under the command of any one governor, he proposed to reduce the opportunities for revolt. The power and the prestige of the equestrian class were enlarged at the expense of the Senate, and the prefect of the Praetorian Guard was given a greater sphere of activity, especially in judicial affairs. Soon the office came to be held by leading jurists rather than by military men. By a careful reorganization of finances, by increasing taxes and expanding greatly the system of requisitions, Septimius was able not merely to restore the credit of the state which had been almost destroyed by Commodus' senseless extravagances, but also to leave an enormous fortune to his successors.

The most significant reforms of Septimius were military. He increased the number of legions, made the conditions of service more attractive, and lowered the old barriers between praetorian and legionary, officer and enlisted man, army and civil service. Septimius scrapped the old Praetorian Guard, which had been recruited from Italians and Roman citizens from the older provinces, and created a new guard for which legionaries from any part of the Empire were eligible. Any soldier might now aspire to service in the praetorians and eventually to an officer's commission, for which such service was a prerequisite. Since the common soldier could become an officer and the officer in turn a civil servant, the highest military and civil offices in the state were potentially open to any loyal and able enlisted man. But there were dangers in this seeming democratization of the army and the civil service. Army officers, elevated to the hierarchy of bureaucrats, had no real experience in civil affairs, no conception of the Principate as a civil government. They thought rather in terms of military rule, and their methods were those of men who had spent their lives in the army with its traditions of discipline and force.

By recruiting legionaries and praetorians on a broader basis and by stationing a permanent legionary garrison for the first time in Italy itself, the emperor tried to break down some of the distinctions that still separated Italy from the provinces. Italy was now being assimilated to the rank of the provinces. Troops were recruited increasingly from the peasantry and from the frontier provinces, which had been only superficially Romanized. The army, to be sure, was neither a class-conscious peasant army at war with the urban elements of the Empire nor a barbarian force bent on destroying Rome from within, but Rome was depending to a dangerous extent upon men whose understanding of the Roman tradition was slight and whose devotion to it was less than their interest in their own gain. More and more the Augustan Principate was giving way to military rule. An eloquent epitome of the new conception of government is to be found in Septimius' last words of advice to his sons: "Enrich the soldiers and scorn the world."

The Successors of Septimius Severus

These tendencies continued during the reign of Septimius' son, cruel Caracalla (211–217). In 212 the new emperor issued his famous edict (*Constitutio Antoniniana*) conferring Roman citizenship upon practically all the subjects of the Empire. This was the logical culmination of a process which even before the Antonine Age had resulted in the leveling of many of the distinctions between Romans and provincials. The edict, however, was no disinterested act of generosity, for it provided a greater number of taxpayers. Even this expedient was not enough to balance a budget reduced by lavish gifts to troops and favorites, bribes and subsidies to barbarians, and an extravagant building program. By tampering with the currency, Caracalla made it possible for the state to weather the storm, but the depreciation of the coinage proved to be no permanent solution to a chronic condition.

Again and again the soldiers showed their power. After the death of Caracalla, the troops placed his assassin on the throne, only to pull him down a few months later. Then they proclaimed as emperor a psychopathic boy of fifteen who, after four years of misrule, was murdered by the Praetorian Guard and replaced by a worthier relative. In 227, however, not only did a new danger arise on Rome's eastern borders when a revived Persian empire replaced the Parthians as her most dangerous enemies; but throughout the length of the Empire's northern frontier—from the Rhine to the Black Sea—swarms of barbarians breached the undermanned defenses, crossed the Rhine and the Danube, and threatened Italy itself. When the emperor attempted to buy off the invaders, the troops who had once hailed him slew him and gave the imperial purple to one of their own number, a Thracian peasant who had risen from the ranks (235). The Severan dynasty, which had been founded by Septimius Severus in 193 and to which his successors belonged at least nominally, was now ended.

Septimius Severus had kept in hand the soldiers to whom he owed his throne. The troops, however, soon learned their strength, and as their insubordination increased, imperial power steadily decayed. Eager for gifts and higher pay, the soldiers were prepared to support their candidate only as long as he pandered to their greed. When he failed, they transferred their allegiance to another. Thus the army controlled the emperors, whose policies were increasingly dictated by the need to appease this powerful pressure group. In these circumstances the Empire could not long escape chaos and disintegration.

All the resources of a static if not a shrinking economy had to be tapped for money to pay the army for its support, to pay bribes to enemies who could not be defeated, and to meet the expenses of a bureaucracy which mushroomed as the central government assumed powers and functions once conceded to the municipalities. An immense hierarchy of civil servants was created to collect money, exact goods and services, and in general maintain the emperor's despotic rule. The normal revenues of the state were insufficient, and the system of compulsory services, employed sporadically in the past, was expanded by the Severan dynasty. The government imposed intolerable burdens upon town and country. From Egypt, Asia Minor, Africa, and the Rhineland came complaints that the people were being reduced to poverty and desperation by heavier taxes and an oppressive system of forced services and requisitions. Moreover, individuals and cities which had supported an unsuccessful aspirant for imperial power were punished by the victor. The provinces became full of homeless men, ruined peasants and businessmen, deserters from the army, political refugees, and victims of an emperor's vengefulness who joined themselves in rebel bands and eked out a precarious livelihood by brigandage. Under Septimius Severus, it is true, certain parts of the Empire especially favored by the ruler enjoyed prosperity and their cities and inhabitants were treated well. Clearly, however, their privileges depended upon the whims and interests of one man and could be withdrawn as arbitrarily as they had been granted.

Military Anarchy under the Soldier-Emperors

With the passing of the Severan dynasty in 235, the Roman Empire was ruled for fifty years by a bewildering succession of soldier-emperors, elevated to office by their troops and dethroned by them or by the army of a rival. Of twenty-six reigning emperors during that half-century only one escaped violent death. Some lasted only a few months or less, nearly none for more than seven years. Most of these military adventurers were of provincial birth and some were of peasant stock. Most of them had risen through the ranks and were able and doughty soldiers; but trained in the army, they were generally ignorant of the older Roman conception of a civilian state. The real capital of the Empire was no longer Rome, but the headquarters of the general who momentarily held the throne. Government was by military decree, and terroristic methods were enforced by a swarm of secret agents, spies, and informers. Some of the emperors were competent leaders and organizers, but preoccupied as they were with domestic and foreign enemies, they had little opportunity to display their administrative skill. A contemporary observer, St. Cyprian, bishop of Carthage, gives us a somber and revealing picture of the misery and despair of this world in crisis: "Behold, the roads closed by brigands, the sea blocked by pirates, the bloodshed and horror of universal strife. The world drips with mutual slaughter, and murder, considered a crime when perpetrated by individuals, is regarded as virtuous when committed publicly." [2] Thus the *Pax Romana* dissolved in a half-century of military anarchy.

Rome's defenses on the Rhine, the Danube, and in the East were breached by enemies who took advantage of the private wars of the Roman armies and overran undefended provinces. The recent creation of a new Persian empire under Ardashir, founder of the dynasty called Sassanian after a reputed ancestor, Sassan, raised a dangerous rival to Rome's eastern power. Under his son, Sapor or Shapur (241–272), the Sassanian Empire almost destroyed Roman authority in the East. In the north, Gothic and other German invaders intensified their pressure and flung themselves across the frontiers to carry their raids into the heart of the Empire. These simultaneous attacks were almost fatal. By the middle of the century the northern frontier was shattered; barbarians poured into Italy and swept over the provinces of Gaul and Spain. The Goths took to the sea and sacked cities on the Black Sea and the Aegean. Under their Sassanian rulers, the Persians occupied Mesopotamia and Syria and all Asia seemed lost. When the emperors could not defeat these enemies, they bought peace or a respite from attack by paying tribute to them. Rome's prestige at home and abroad was lowered by this policy of appeasement.

Famine and plague rode side by side with Rome's enemies. The scourge of epidemic disease raged for fifteen years, decimating whole regions and undermining the Empire's already weakened powers of resistance. As law and order

[2] Cyprian, *Letters*, I, 6.

broke down, the seas were infested with pirates, the roads
with brigands. In various parts of the Empire there were
terrible peasant revolts, as the poor were driven from their
homes by invading barbarians, undisciplined troops, and
voracious tax collectors. A swarm of warlords, the so-called
Thirty Tyrants, appeared in almost every province and
the unity of the Empire collapsed. If some of these pre-
tenders were speedily suppressed, others maintained themselves for a number of years in independence of the central
government. Postumus, a governor of Gaul, organized that
province, Spain, and Britain as a separate empire of the
Gauls. Almost simultaneously, the romantic queen Zenobia,
ruler of the caravan city of Palmyra, a Roman vassal kingdom in the northern Arabian Desert, usurped Rome's control of a huge area in the East. By 268 large sections of the
Empire were in the hands of such rebels or barbarians and
Persians. Ironically Gallienus, the reigning Roman emperor,
chose for one of his coins the legend *Ubique Pax*, "Peace
Everywhere."

Recovery under Claudius Gothicus and Aurelian

The work of recovery was begun in 268 by the emperor
Claudius Gothicus, who so soundly defeated the Goths that
they ceased to be a problem for nearly a century. His heroic
efforts were continued by Aurelian (270–275), an outstanding general and able administrator who was chosen, like his
predecessors, by the army. He defeated the German invaders
of Italy, rioters in Rome, and the rebel kingdoms of Palmyra
and Gaul. The barbarians were driven back, but in their
wake they left terrible devastation, burned and looted cities
and heavy casualties. Once-flourishing cities became mere
shadows of themselves. In Gaul, Autun shrank from nearly

500 acres to fewer than 25, Bordeaux from 175 to 56, and by A.D. 300 hardly a city in Gaul had an area greater than 60 acres. By 260, Alexandria in Egypt, remote though it was from raids, lost some 60 per cent of its former population to plague and famine. Because of Rome's limited resources of men and money, Aurelian evacuated the province of Dacia, and once again the Danube was fixed as the northern frontier. In the interior of the Empire, cities which had relied for centuries upon the *Pax Romana*, enforced by loyal armies, hastily improvised defensive walls. Rome itself, which had enjoyed security for over 650 years, was ringed by a massive wall.

Defense by Tribute

Great quantities of money which the Empire could ill afford had been paid to the Germans and Persians as booty, ransom, or tribute. In the dark days of the 60's, the emperors had resorted to the costly and dangerous policy of buying the services of barbarian war bands, in order to replenish the Roman forces depleted by plague and war. Farming, trade, and industry had suffered; peasants, workers, and the urban middle class were in despair and groaned under the burden of taxes and requisitions. It is a revealing glimpse into the decline of commerce and the general prosperity of cities that between 235 and 253, 83 cities of Asia Minor issued their last known coins, and between 253 and 268, 107 more apparently ceased to issue coins. The imperial coinage had been repeatedly debased until it was worthless, prices had soared, the standard of living had declined. Such was Rome's melancholy plight in 275, but at least the integrity of the Empire had been restored by Aurelian, *Restitutor Orbis*, "Restorer of the World."

A half-century of chaos had nearly run its course. The army and the generals whom it had placed on the throne had ruled the Empire and dictated its policies. The state had become a military monarchy, worse, a military anarchy. To satisfy the wishes of the soldiers all else had been sacrificed, for their support was needed if the emperor himself was to survive. An undisciplined, insubordinate soldiery, more interested in distributing political power and gaining its rewards than in fighting the enemy, had become an incubus upon the civil population. The army, preoccupied with the game of emperor-making, had paid only scant attention to the protection of the Empire, and the generals, bidding for the imperial purple, still further disorganized the defenses, which broke down under the strain of simultaneous attack on two fronts.

Economic Crisis

Military anarchy was accompanied by economic crisis. Ruinous methods were devised to meet the expenses of government. Gifts to the soldiers to ensure their loyalty, doles to the populace of Rome, the personal extravagance of emperors, an expanding bureaucracy, the high cost of civil and foreign wars, bribes and tribute to the enemy, the devastation caused by invaders, all these had drained the wealth of the Empire. Already in the Antonine Age, as we have seen, there were ominous signs that the once-flourishing cities were finding it difficult to satisfy the demands imposed upon them by the imperial government. Now the heavy hand of the centralized bureaucracy oppressed rural districts and cities alike. Hardly a class was exempt from the financial and personal obligations which were ruthlessly exacted by the agents and officials of the emperor. The system of compulsory requisitions was extended to pay the soaring costs of defense and administration. In addition to regular taxes, the rich were expected to make money contributions; others were to perform manual labor on the maintenance of aqueducts and public buildings, or to provide oil and grain, or to transport goods, supplies, and soldiers. The burden weighed most oppressively upon the urban propertied classes from which the local magistrates and senators were drawn. As greater demands were made upon their dwindling resources, municipal office, once an honor eagerly sought and willingly held, became indistinguishable from a compulsory public service. To make sure that necessary activities were performed for city and state, the central government intervened to keep the offices filled and thereby undermined local autonomy. Certain people received exemptions by doing other work of public utility, but the more persons were granted the privilege, the greater was the burden on their less fortunate fellows. In the end the constant requisitions upon their capital led to the impoverishment of the middle class, which had been one of the main pillars of the economic structure of the Empire. The cities which had been the keystone of Graeco-Roman civilization declined with the middle class.

The rural districts were no more fortunate. Farmers sought to escape onerous taxes and requisitions by abandoning their farms and taking to the roads as highwaymen. Large areas of land went out of cultivation and the burden was all the more crushing for those who remained. Orders were now given to town councils to make up the deficit of taxes on deserted farms, and landowners were compelled to take up abandoned farms adjoining theirs and to produce enough to pay the taxes on them.

Administrative Abuses

As early as the time of the Antonines, communities had complained to the central government about the requisitions demanded by imperial officials. Inscriptions and papyri documents now reveal the rising tide of protests against these abuses. The very frequency of imperial edicts designed to mitigate these evils shows how ineffective they were. So useful a device for obtaining money and services was not easily abandoned. From Egypt, Syria, Asia Minor, Africa, and Thrace comes evidence of the acute distress caused by the imposition of these burdens. In Egypt officials and soldiers requisitioned boats, pack animals, and drivers for the transport of troops and supplies, as well as grain and other foodstuffs, clothing, and leather hides. For visits of prefects or the emperor and his retinue on tours of inspection there were special requisitions of transportation, food, and housing; for the upkeep of the imperial post service, farmers' horses were pressed into service and farmers themselves forced to labor to maintain roads and stations. Small wonder that the Egyptians fled from their villages to the swamps of the Nile Delta in order to escape these intolerable exactions. Syrian villagers complained to the governor that they had been forced to furnish lodging for soldiers and officials. The Thracians objected to soldiers and provincial administrators who demanded the right of being entertained at the expense of the community. In Asia Minor tenants on imperial estates complained that they were being ruined by the high cost of entertaining representatives of the government or by heavy fines and other burdens, as well as by the exactions of soldiers and public officials, who demanded the services of the villagers and their oxen for transport duty. To escape, they had been forced to bribe these officials, and when they had been unable to produce enough some of them had been imprisoned, others even executed. Farm work was at a standstill; no alternative remained but to abandon the imperial domains unless the emperor intervened in their behalf. Thus the Roman world was filled with harassed and uprooted men from town and country. The stock questions put to an oracle in Egypt are revealing: "Am I to become a beggar?" "Is my flight to be stopped?" "Shall I be sold?" "Shall I have to be a member of the local council?"

By regulation and regimentation the government tried to stem its financial difficulties; these multiplied as one domestic crisis succeeded another and as enemies pressed upon the Roman frontiers. The need for money to provide gifts for the legions, the high cost of defensive wars which did not pay for themselves in land and booty, the heavy toll of taxpayers taken by war and disease, the disorganization of business and farming, the loss of revenue from lost provinces, the draining away of Rome's shrinking store of precious metals for unproductive luxury goods—all these factors complicated a desperate situation. Rome had ceased to expand and had no great new fields to exploit. Instead she had to depend upon her internal resources and these, as they were organized, were inadequate. The repeatedly tried solution of debasing the currency and increasing the amount in circulation had a disastrous effect upon economic life. The gold coinage lost all stability and the silver coins lost 98 per cent of their silver content; records from the Roman province of Egypt indicate that banks, which there as elsewhere in the Empire carried on many of the operations which we associate with banking, refused to accept the imperial coinage. The market was now flooded with this worthless silver-washed currency, and a catastrophic inflation was the result. The price of grain doubled between A.D. 250 and 265, and as prices climbed the purchasing power of such trust funds as the *alimenta* shrank to the vanishing point. The "alimentary" system, established by the emperor Nerva (96–98) and expanded by his successors, granted state loans to Italian small landowners at moderate interest payments which were set aside for the support of needy children. The interest from the *alimenta* was now worth about 2 per cent of its original purchasing power. Under these inflationary conditions millions were impoverished and utterly wretched. Only the soldiers, imperial officials, and rich landlords enjoyed relative security. The state itself was virtually bankrupt. In Gibbon's phrase, it "appeared every day less formidable to its enemies, more odious and oppressive to its subjects."

Intellectual Activity of the Third Century

Confused and chaotic though the century was, it was not completely barren of intellectual activity. If there were no outstanding writers and no great art, there were at least competent writers and artists, while in religion and philosophy there were vital stirrings as men looked for faith and hope in a world which was uncertain and insecure, full of darkness and despair. There were still schools and universities, and the curriculum, based upon Greek and Latin classics, was little changed. Philosophy retained its primacy in some centers, and everywhere rhetoric and law were emphasized. In jurisprudence, the field which Rome had made peculiarly her own, important work was done by some of the greatest jurists in a long and distinguished line. The third-century jurists Papinian, Ulpian, and Paulus helped elucidate, systematize, and preserve the law which was Rome's richest legacy to the mediaeval world. In science, at the beginning of the period, Galen produced a synthesis of existing medical knowledge which had a remarkable influence upon the history of medicine in the European and Arab world of the Middle Ages. The great age of science had ended long before, however, and pseudoscience and superstition were winning a victory. Never before had the Roman world been so full of charlatans with scientific pretensions, astrologers, soothsayers, wonder-workers, and wizards.

The mass of the people, dispirited and depressed, found hope in magic and superstition or in ancient cults, Oriental mystery religions, and Christianity. A few intellectuals, dissatisfied with the Stoicism and Epicureanism which had flourished under the Late Republic and Early Empire, found answers in Neoplatonism, which was the leading philosophy of the pagan world until the sixth century. Its chief figure was the Egyptian-born Plotinus (c.205–270) who settled in Rome during the period of military anarchy. His work, the *Enneads*, or *Nine Volumes*, was edited by Porphyry, the best known of his disciples. Neoplatonism was a synthesis of Platonic, Aristotelian, Stoic, and other philosophic elements adjusted to the religious aspirations of the time. By thought and meditation the Neoplatonists sought to be in touch with the absolute, with the eternal, which they conceived as lying behind all phenomena. It was the Neoplatonists who in the last centuries of the Empire defended the classical intellectual tradition against Christian critics. Christian thought itself was ultimately influenced by this last great school of pagan thought.

Even in the darkest days of the century, sculptors, painters, and architects continued their activities, and when material conditions improved somewhat, as a result of the reorganization of the Empire at the end of the century, fresh opportunities were given them. There was still originality, especially in architecture, a fair degree of technical skill, a sense of color and decoration revealed in mosaics and sarcophagi, and strength displayed notably in portrait busts. Judged by the standards of classical art, however, the art of the period lacked originality, realism, balance, and proportion. More generally than in the Augustan period it was imitative, conventional, showy, and tasteless. In this mediocre art of late Rome, however, may be found the germs of Christian art of East and West in mediaeval Europe.

In literature there were new interests as the reading public sought relaxation and escape from care. The Greek romantic novels, the *Aethiopica* by Heliodorus or *Daphnis and Chloe* by Longus, with their rather stereotyped themes of love and adventure and their exotic settings or charming descriptions of the quiet pastoral life, enjoyed popularity. With the exception of Dio Cassius, who early in the third century wrote a *Roman History* in eighty books, there was no outstanding historian, but other writers produced historical biography and did antiquarian research. Much useful, if unoriginal, work was done in collecting anthologies of earlier writings and in literary criticism. In general, the authors of the time were pedantic and artificial, more interested in the arrangement of words, the external form, than in content and substance. A wealth of rhetorical adornment scarcely concealed their poverty of ideas. Christian literature in Greek and Latin was more austerely practical. Its themes were religion and theology, its emphases polemical and defensive, as Christianity itself fought for survival. For the pagan writers of a civilization in crisis originality flagged and the creative spirit waned. The future belonged to the writers, as well as the artists and thinkers, of a religion which was slowly winning its way in a still-hostile world.

Diocletian and Constantine the Great: Administrative Reforms

In 275 Aurelian was assassinated and several emperors succeeded him in the familiar pattern of rulers created and deposed by their armies. Finally, Diocletian (284–305), the last of the military adventurers of the century, was given the imperial throne by his troops. Diocletian, an Illyrian of humble birth who had risen from the ranks of the army through military ability, was no mere soldier, but an administrator of unusual power. His reign marked the end of half a century of military anarchy and the beginning of a new epoch in Rome's declining career. His reorganization of the Empire, carried several stages farther by his successor Constantine the Great (306–337), gave the state a new lease on life.

These reforming emperors restored the unity of the Empire and established a measure of peace, stability, and security, but the price of survival was high and the results impermanent. For the little that remained of the relatively liberal Augustan Principate there was substituted a hereditary despotism. A free economy was replaced by a state-controlled one. The inhabitants of the Empire were regimented: workers were frozen in their occupations, farmers tied to the land, and city officials to their posts. The reorganization, to be sure, was not revolutionary; rather it made systematic and permanent emergency measures which had been taken during the years of crisis. Under Diocletian and Constantine the Roman government became an undisguised absolutism, but this was merely the logical conclusion of a process which had been developing for at least a century.

Since the problems of defense and administration seemed too great for any one ruler, Diocletian sought a formula which would preserve the unity of the Empire, maintain his own autocratic power, and provide an orderly succession of emperors without the intervention of the army. He divided the Empire into eastern and western portions and appointed a colleague to rule the West, while he governed the East and exercised a general control over both halves. Each of these Augusti adopted a Caesar to assist in the management of imperial affairs and eventually to succeed him. The government was now divided among four rulers, two in the East and two in the West. Each had his own capital, army, praetorian prefect, and bureaucracy. This scheme, with its provision for automatic succession, broke down after Diocletian's abdication in 305, however, and there was a resumption of civil war as the Augusti and Caesars fought each other. The victor, Constantine, son of one of Diocletian's Caesars and probably like Diocletian himself of Illyrian origin, won the western provinces first and finally the whole Empire for himself.

The New Ceremonial

The emperor's own person was surrounded by an aura of sacrosanctity. He was no longer *princeps*, first citizen of the state, but *dominus et deus*, lord master and god. From the Sassanian Empire was borrowed an elaborate court cere-

monial with all the Oriental trappings of an imperial ward-
robe, luxurious raiment, and a diadem. To impress the ex-
alted station of the emperor upon ordinary mortals and to
emphasize the distance which separated him from them, the
few subjects who were granted audiences with the sacred
ruler had to prostrate themselves before him and kiss the
hem of his robe. These were a few of the externals of imperial office which the Byzantine emperors in the East and
the kings of western Europe eventually inherited.

Military Reforms

The emperor's power, however, depended upon more
than ceremonial. The army had to be reduced to subservi-
ence, the administration of the provinces reorganized, the
bureaucracy made more efficient, and the economic strength
of the Empire restored.

One of the great weaknesses of Rome in the preceding
years had been her inability to fight simultaneously on two
fronts; she needed a larger army if she were to resist the
twin menace of barbarian and Persian. But any expansion
of the army increased the potential danger of a *coup d'état*
like those which had almost destroyed Rome during the
past half-century. The risk was taken and the number of
troops increased, but their organization and distribution
were changed. The army, consisting now of about 650,000
men, was divided into two main branches: a garrison force
(*limitanei* and *riparii*), stationed along the frontiers, and
expeditionary forces (*comitatenses*), posted at various strategic locations from which they could be quickly moved
to danger zones on the frontier. Strong palace guards (*pala-
tini*) protected the emperor himself. Cavalry units were
enlarged and given a far more important role than they

had hitherto. When the need arose, the frontier garrisons were reinforced by hired warriors from barbarian tribes in treaty relations with Rome. This reorganization of the army nearly doubled the number of effective troops, and more officers had to be provided. Many of them came up through the ranks, since a steady sequence of promotions made it possible for an enlisted man to win a commission and eventually even command of a whole army. In the new army the most important role, that of fighting the invaders, was given to barbarians. The plague and civil wars had so reduced the available manpower of the Empire that the only solution seemed to be to use Germans to fight other Germans. The sequel showed that the barbarians, to whom land or money was given in return for military service, could not be trusted to defend an empire to which they had no genuine attachment.

Separation of Military and Administrative Functions

Diocletian almost entirely dissociated the civil service from the army. The sole concern of the troops was to defend the Empire; the business of the bureaucracy was to administer it for the emperor and above all to collect the taxes. To assure more efficient administration and to weaken the capacity of governors to revolt, the provinces were divided and subdivided until by the fifth century there were about 120. These tiny provinces—and Italy itself had shrunk to provincial status—were grouped in larger administrative districts called dioceses, each under a *vicarius*, and the dioceses in turn were assigned by Diocletian to the Augusti and Caesars. To each of these four rulers was attached a praetorian prefect who was charged with his former judicial powers as well as sweeping administrative functions in connection with public utilities and services.

Although some of the provincial governors continued to be drawn from the Senate, that body did not have even nominal control over the provinces. It was in fact no more than a municipal council for the city of Rome, and by Constantine's time the distinction between senators and equestrians had disappeared. A host of new officials, many with pompous titles, exercised a vigilant control over the subjects of the Empire. Administrative institutions became more rigid as the conditions which had called them into being worsened. As the expenditures for defense and war mounted, the need for money became more acute, and a complicated and costly machinery of government was devised to enforce the regimentation of the subjects of the state. The Empire was caught in a web from which it could not seem to escape.

This was the administrative framework of the Later Roman Empire. Changes in detail were made by the emperors after Constantine, but it was essentially upon this model of an absolute, bureaucratic state that the Germans formed their kingdoms and the Byzantine emperors built their government. We shall see too that many of these institutions were adopted by the Christian church when it found need for a more complex organization.

Economic Reforms

By their economic reforms Diocletian and Constantine accelerated the process which had already brought the inhabitants of the Empire under the all-embracing control of the state. Not only were the requisitions and compulsory public services reinforced and expanded, but they were also made more systematic and regular. Early in his reign Diocletian tried to end monetary confusion and to stimulate trade by re-establishing a reliable currency in both gold and silver. Prices continued to climb, however, and in 301 the emperor issued the famous Edict of Diocletian which, by setting wage controls and fixing price ceilings for the sale of nearly everything, proposed to eliminate profiteers and black-market activities. Although the death penalty was prescribed for infractions, it proved impossible to enforce the edict, which made no distinction between wholesale and retail prices and no allowance for differences in quality or variations in supply and demand. In the eastern provinces the edict caused serious riots, and after a year or so it became a dead letter; while in the West it does not seem to have been effectively enforced at all. This attempt to combat inflation was as unsuccessful as his currency reform. Both were palliatives which might bring temporary relief, but could not cure a deep-seated malady.

Diocletian and Constantine established a "planned economy" not because of a doctrinaire preference, but because they were hard pressed to obtain two basic and closely related requirements, men and money. Incessant civil and foreign wars, famine and epidemic, a declining birth rate, and a high rate of infant mortality had created a serious shortage of manpower which became more critical as the emperors expanded the army and civil service. There was a need for men not only to perform vital public services, but also to produce the food, clothing, and other products which the state and its inhabitants required. Above all, men were needed to provide the taxes without which the state would perish. We have already seen that the government had to have money to pay the army and the bureaucracy, to appease potential enemies, and to meet the high costs of an Orientalized court and an ambitious building program. The scheme of economic reorganization was a drastic solution for a complicated problem.

A new system of taxation, a tax in kind (*annona*) levied on land and the labor employed upon it, largely replaced the tax in money. The new tax varied according to the productive capacity of the land and the number of men working upon it. Since it was payable in kind, the government had to have state granaries and stockyards and new officials to care for them. If the tax were to be paid, the land had to be kept under cultivation and farmers had to be prevented from abandoning their work, as many had been doing. First the tenant farmers (*coloni*) on imperial estates and eventually those on private estates were compelled to remain on their lands for life. Finally the order was applied to their heirs as well. In this way farm workers were tied to the soil and an important step had been taken toward reducing them to serfdom. Many small landowners accepted the same status voluntarily, for when they fell heavily into debt they could "commend" themselves to wealthier landlords who paid their debts and in return took them over as *coloni* for life.

No one escaped the ubiquitous state. City-dwellers, both workers and businessmen, had to pay regular taxes in money and in kind, an oppressive special tax collected every five years, and emergency taxes payable in labor or produce. When certain essential workers, for example, members of the various associations or *collegia* of millers, grain shippers, bakers, and butchers, tried to leave their occupations in order to avoid the demands of the state, they were compelled to remain. Workers who had found employment elsewhere were forced back to their former occupations, and finally the children of workers and merchants were bound to their fathers' callings. Under Constantine the principle of hereditary public service was made law and applied to all classes, including soldiers, civil servants, and municipal officials. In effect, the state had nationalized everyone and everything.

Diocletian and Constantine performed a herculean task. By their reorganization they gave the Roman Empire a respite from invasions and civil war, but the respite was brief and its price very high. No adequate resistance was likely to be offered to the barbarian invaders by a people who had lost freedom and hope and, above all, their belief in the cause of Rome. Roman civilization had been based upon an association of self-governing city-states under the protection of the *Pax Romana*. It could not remain unchanged when local government, whose vitality had already begun to ebb in the second century, was given its death blow by the establishment of a centralized, absolute state. The decline of the Roman Empire, which we shall analyze in a later chapter, was both postponed and accelerated by Diocletian and Constantine.

The Beginning of a New Era

Two acts of Constantine the Great may well be considered as symbolizing the end of one phase of history and the beginning of another. His conversion to Christianity marks the change from a declining pagan civilization to a vital Christian civilization, and his establishment of a new Christian capital at Constantinople in place of pagan Rome signifies the shift of the center of gravity from West to East. The Roman Empire in the West endured for nearly a century and a half before the barbarian invaders built their kingdoms upon its ruins. In the East the Byzantine or Eastern Roman Empire, whose foundations were laid when Constantine created Constantinople, played a major role in history for another thousand years. In both East and West, Roman civilization was the matrix for those institutional and cultural forms which we call mediaeval.

CHAPTER III

The Ordeal and Triumph

of Christianity

THE conversion of the emperor Constantine the Great to Christianity marked the beginning of a new epoch. A religion which had been derided and persecuted now won its way to victory over the other religions in the Empire, the older Graeco-Roman gods as well as the new cults brought in from the East. In the twilight hours of the Empire the pagan gods went down to defeat, and the triumph of Christianity heralded the birth of the Middle Ages.

What were the factors within Christianity which fostered its victory? What were the external circumstances which facilitated its spread from a tiny and insignificant part of the Roman Empire over the length and breadth of that immense Roman world? Why was the imperial government, normally tolerant in matters of religion, hostile to Christianity? Although it is difficult, perhaps impossible, to answer categorically questions which concern men's spiritual attachments and aspirations, an examination of religious developments during the first three or four centuries of the Empire may at least suggest some possible explanations of both the ordeal and the triumph of Christianity. Without such an inquiry neither the later Roman Empire nor the early Middle Ages can be understood.

Decline of Stoicism

We have seen how in the face of overwhelming material difficulties the Romans sought comfort in religion or consolation in philosophy. In Stoicism or in the more recent Neoplatonism a handful of intellectuals found a formula which resolved their problems. But philosophy failed to answer the psychological needs of the mass of the people, even if, like Neoplatonism, it adopted some of the panoply of religion. It offered few rays of hope regarding either the grim present or the uncertain future, and it provided no colorful ceremony to compensate for the drabness of life. If it addressed itself to the intellect, the message of philosophy was too coldly logical and austerely rational to satisfy even the changing interests of intellectuals, let alone the unlettered majority. Philosophy could only flourish by making an alliance with religion, by admitting some divine and supernatural power into its system. The Graeco-Roman spirit of rationalism was being buffeted and broken by waves of religious enthusiasm. Of all the many changes occuring in the Roman Empire, this change from a scientific, objective, and rational basis of thought and life to a way of life based upon faith and dogma is perhaps the most revolutionary. The emphasis shifted from this world to a world to come, from an attempt by man to solve his own problems to a reliance upon a higher power. Simultaneously with the disintegration of the Empire, both cause and result of that collapse, the ancient tradition of science and rationalism crumbled.

The fate of Stoic philosophy in the Later Empire is instructive. Here was a philosophy which was fundamentally monotheistic, teaching that there is in the universe an immortal all-pervasive world-soul of whose divinity each man possesses a spark. From this was deduced the universal brotherhood of mankind long before Christianity reached the same conclusions. In this sense it can be said that Stoicism drew a blueprint of the universal empire Rome was to form. Its code of ethics was of the loftiest, its ideal of conduct austere, and it formed some of the noblest characters in Roman history. Stoic insistence that the prince is not the lord, but the servant of his people, and that his duty to them is an obligation from God anticipates what is nowadays called enlightened despotism. This conception was the foundation of policy under the Antonines and it influenced their enlightened predecessors.

There are in Stoicism obvious similarities and parallels to religious thought, and particularly to Christian thought. These were close enough to make it possible for Christians in the Middle Ages to claim that Seneca, the famous Stoic of the first century, had corresponded with St. Paul and had received his ideas from him. Perhaps the simplest way to discover how this belief could come about is to read the *Meditations* of the Stoic emperor Marcus Aurelius with one's Bible at hand. And it is this strongly religious aspect which explains why, as the traditional and official Graeco-Roman religion began to lose its hold on the upper classes, Stoicism could fill the vacuum for a time. This role, however, was strictly limited by the character of Stoicism itself. It was cold and detached, directed essentially to the mind, not to the heart and spirit; it concentrated upon this world and held out no hopes for the next; it was no longer at its best, but had moved in the direction of religious mysticism.

The great schools of philosophy were still open—they were not closed until 529—but they proved unable to prevent infiltration from the Orient, particularly of pseudosciences like astrology and its more degraded fellow, magic, and along with them an irrationality and a tawdry mysticism quite alien to the original character of Greek philosophy as it appears in Socrates, Plato, Aristotle, and Zeno, the founder of Stoicism.

For the less educated, that is, for the masses within the Empire, formal Greek philosophy must have been largely a closed book. Some sort of "downward infiltration" of the major concepts of this body of thought, however, seems to have occured on a fairly important scale and apparently gave life to the formal Roman state religion. But when the gradual erosion of belief in the traditional gods began to affect this lower section of society, it left the same kind of spiritual vacuum that it had among the upper classes.

Graeco-Roman Gods, Emperor-Worship, and Oriental Mystery Cults

There were still the gods of the Graeco-Roman pantheon, Jupiter, Juno, Minerva, Mars, and others, which continued for long to enjoy the favor of the state and formed, indeed, part of the official state religion. More important was the cult of the deified emperors which was fostered by the government. In the eastern half of the Empire, where such practices had a long history, the reigning emperor was sometimes worshiped as a living god, but until the third century divine honors were only accorded by the Senate to the emperor after his death. In any event, by acknowledging the divinity of their rulers, the people in the provinces as in Rome expressed their loyalty to the Empire over whose destinies the deified emperors presided. Emperor-worship, however, while it might serve as a powerful cement binding the disparate people of the Empire together in common devotion to the divine symbol of the state, satisfied few of the emotional and spiritual needs of mankind. The imperial cult was official and formal, cold and impersonal. It emphasized the subject's obligations to the state and its gods; it had no real appeal for human hearts. Men craved for a religion which would satisfy their individual aspirations and lighten the burden of existence. Since the Roman government permitted its subjects to worship whatever gods they wished, provided they also rendered homage to the gods of Rome, the imperial cult was no bar to the spread of other religions, and new gods helped fill the spiritual void.

The ancient household gods, the Lares and Penates, were still ever-present and worthy of devotion, while other gods of an earlier day continued to hold the favor of many in town and country. As men sought solace and help, there was, in fact, a revival of interest in half-forgotten local and national gods. Some Romans, especially in the humbler sections of society, fell back on ritual duties to gods far older than the receding ancestral gods of Rome, upon nature gods and fertility gods dating from the most primitive times. These survived in a bewildering array of local variations, although with a considerable common denominator of fundamental likeness. Such deities have an extraordinary appeal to simple folk and for this reason are almost indestructible. In the Roman Empire they had an especial appeal because they were identified with a timeless local tradition and sentiment far older than any rival the Empire itself had to offer.

In the second place the common folk of the Empire could turn to importations from abroad—almost wholly from the

Orient, the mother of religions. In general, the old gods of Rome lost popularity and were eclipsed by foreign gods, who reached out especially from the eastern provinces to attract a wider following. From Egypt came the Graeco-Oriental gods Isis and Sarapis; from Asia Minor Magna Mater, or the Great Mother Goddess; from Syria various deities, especially Sol Invictus, the Invincible Sun; and from Persia came Mithras.

Of all the Oriental gods which invaded the West, Mithras, militant god of the sun, was the most notable and perhaps the most formidable rival with which Christianity had to contend. From the earlier Zoroastrian religion of the Persian Empire, Mithraism adopted the idea of an eternal struggle between Ahura Mazda, god of light and goodness, and Ahriman, god of darkness and evil. Mithras was conceived by his followers as a warrior leading them in battle in behalf of Ahura Mazda. Long before our period of the Empire, Mithraism and the other eastern cults had spread beyond the confines of their homeland, gained a foothold in Rome and the western half of the Empire, and won great numbers of proselytes. As a civic duty men still worshiped the gods of the state, but they expressed their inmost personal faith by their devotion to the mystery cults. Rome had conquered the East; now she was being conquered by the gods of the East.

The Spread of the Mystery Cults

The unity of the Empire, the relative ease of communications, and the freedom of movement assured by the *Pax Romana* facilitated the spread of the Oriental religions. Even in Republican times slaves and freemen, migrating from Greece and the Near East, had brought their gods with

them. Under the Empire, as men traveled from one end of
the Roman world to another, they helped propagate their
religious beliefs. When they came west for business or to
establish their residence, merchants and craftsmen from the
Graeco-Oriental portions of the Empire continued to worship their native gods. So, too, when they were transferred
to the West, soldiers of eastern origin or soldiers who had
been stationed in the East and had there become devotees
of native deities carried their gods with them. Their favorite
was Mithras, whose military qualities naturally appealed to
them. Wherever Roman troops were posted, they established shrines in honor of the warrior god, as abundant
archaeological remains attest.

In general, as we have seen, the Roman government raised
no objections to these alien cults. As long as their rites were
not grossly immoral and as long as their devotees remained
loyal to Rome and formally recognized the gods of the
state and above all the cult of the deified emperor, their gods
were tolerated. Indeed, several eastern religions won official
recognition, and emperors themselves were sometimes fer-
vent and even fanatical worshipers of the Oriental gods. As
early as the Second Punic War, the Republican government
had established at Rome the cult of the Great Mother Goddess of Asia Minor, and from time to time other eastern
cults, notably that of Sol Invictus in the third century A.D.,
had won official favor, although at other times the state had
banned or restricted the practice of such religions at Rome.
When the government took such action, however, it was
because it regarded these religions as a danger to public
morals or a threat to the security of the state.

For their part the Oriental gods were neither jealous of
one another nor mutually exclusive, and adherence to the

cult of one did not preclude devotion to another. A man might worship several gods, the ancient Olympians, Isis and Sarapis, Mithras, and always of course the deified emperors. In time, as the similarity of attributes of various gods came to be recognized, a process of syncretism began to take place, that is, attempts were made to reconcile and fuse different cults into something like a pagan monotheism. In the later third century, Sol Invictus, the Unconquered Sun, was widely recognized as a sovereign and universal deity whose particular attributes were revealed in the many local and individual cults of the Empire. Various emperors paid honor to the god, and Aurelian officially recognized the worship of the sun as a state cult. Although the victory of Christianity rendered this attempt to create a pagan monotheism abortive, the tentative beginnings in this direction indicate the essential tolerance displayed by Rome and her subjects toward religious innovations.

The Appeal of the New Cults

These circumstances provide only part of the explanation for the extraordinary popularity of the Oriental mystery religions. Despite the freedom and facility of movement, official toleration and active encouragement, the foreign gods would not have flourished so strongly unless men had been ready and eager to accept them. We have already seen how in the dark days of the third century, and even earlier under the deceptive tranquillity of the Antonine Age, men had turned to religions which offered divine aid and solace in this troubled world and a promise of redemption and a better life to come in the future. Most of these cults, whose devotees were drawn largely but not exclusively from the lower and middle classes, were secret societies to which members were admitted only after a ritual of initiation. Upon their members they enjoined rigid rules of conduct which helped to bind them together. Their rites of worship gave the devotees an emotional satisfaction which they could not find in the formal and impersonal ceremonies of the civic and state cults. Groping desperately for relief from the misery of the present and seeking to alleviate the pain and burden of life, men eagerly accepted these cults. Their elaborate and sometimes orgiastic ritual and colorful ceremonial relieved the tedium of living and consoled the poor for their poverty. Their organization as societies gave men opportunities for fellowship and a sense of belonging to a group which had common interests and purposes. Above all, the mystery religions provided a respite from intolerable conditions and offered hope of personal immortality to men for whom this life seemed hopeless. Roman society in a time of mounting crisis was ripe for a religious revival, and the Oriental cults, which emphasized a personal and emotional religion, answered men's needs and therefore won a sympathetic reception. Their popularity in the second and third centuries is a measure of the increasing dissatisfaction of men with conditions in the Empire.

The Early Christians

Of the new religions which came in from the Roman East and strove for the allegiance of men, one triumphed over all its rivals and over the Empire itself. This was Christianity, which had its humble origins in the Roman province of Judaea among a group of disciples who soon after the reign of the emperor Augustus gathered around Jesus of Nazareth. At first these disciples addressed themselves to other Jews in Judaea, but soon they began to proselyte in

Jewish communities elsewhere in the East and then in the West, and it was not long before they won converts among devotees of other religions. The greatest of the converts was Paul the Apostle. By his missionary travels and activities he helped to transform a local religion into a universal one with a message for all, pagans as well as Jews. The new religion, however, did not enjoy immediately the popularity of some of the other eastern cults. The first converts were mainly drawn from the humblest class of society, slaves and freemen, from that class in the Roman world which A. J. Toynbee in his stimulating *Study of History* designates as the "internal proletariat," the section of society whose only stake in the Roman community was physical existence. Nevertheless, by the middle of the first century there were Christian groups in every important city in the East, in Rome itself, and probably elsewhere in the West. The *Pax Romana*, the unity of the Mediterranean world, and, above all, the need felt by men for a personal religion to take the place of the impersonal civic religion—these were some of the factors which facilitated the evangelical mission of Paul and others.

The Imperial Attitude toward the Christians

The Christians were ignored at first by the Roman government, which was accustomed to tolerate a host of gods and cults. Rome had granted religious freedom and even civil jurisdiction to the Jews; for a generation this freedom was also enjoyed by the Christians, who were regarded by the Roman government and the people as a Jewish sect. The Christians, however, soon came into conflict with the state. Their unwillingness to participate in the activities of the state, their concentration upon the salvation of the individual, and, above all, their intransigeant refusal to acknowledge the gods of the state and especially the deified emperors even by formal and perfunctory worship made them objects of suspicion. We have noted that participation in the rites of the imperial cult was regarded as a positive test of loyalty to Rome. In contrast to the adherents of other religions which were tolerated by the government, the Christians were uncompromising monotheists. Their refusal to recognize Rome's gods set them off from the devotees of Mithras or Magna Mater and focused the attention of the government upon them. From the Roman point of view, by their unequivocal denial of the divinity of the emperors, the Christians revealed themselves as dangerous public enemies, guilty of disloyalty and treason, or at the very least atheism, since they attacked both the traditional gods of the state and the Oriental gods.

Their organization in societies which had not obtained the approval of the government was another basic reason for the distrust by the government. When the Christians began to develop an organization of their own, they seemed to be building a state within the state. For a long time their converts came from the lower classes of society, and the Christian teachings were regarded as having dangerously radical implications. Persecution, therefore, was not religious but political and stemmed from the desire of the emperors to check insubordination and subversive tendencies and to maintain the unity and integrity of the Empire. Moreover, ordinary men regarded their Christian fellows as clannish and antisocial and accused them of a general "hatred of the human race" or, more specifically, of horrible crimes. From many points of view the Christians seemed to be a disturbing factor in society.

The Persecutions

In 64 the emperor Nero made the Christians scapegoats for the great fire at Rome, and many were put to death after submitting to tortures. In general, however, the imperial government left it to local authorities to deal with the Christians; and during the first two centuries local magistrates or mobs, rather than the central government, were responsible for the sporadic persecution of Christians. The famous correspondence in 112 between the emperor Trajan and Pliny the Younger, his governor in the eastern province of Bithynia, is the classic expression of the official policy of the Roman government. Christians were not to be sought out nor were anonymous accusations to be accepted. If, however, Christians were properly accused and convicted, they were to be punished. "Those, however, who deny their Christianity and prove their denial by praying to our gods, may wipe out past suspicions and secure a free pardon by their recantation."

In the Antonine and Severan periods there was passive tolerance for the Christians or occasional persecution. That many Christians of the second century were permitted to defend their faith by apologetic writings suggests, indeed, a considerable tolerance on the part of the Antonine emperors. The great period of stress for Christianity coincided with the Empire's time of troubles in the third century. Several emperors, especially Decius (249–251), instituted terrible persecutions throughout the Empire, for Christianity had by now become too strong to be dealt with by local authorities. Because of their attitude toward the state and its gods, the Christians seemed to be another of the forces which threatened the breakdown of the Empire in the period of military anarchy. If the unity of the Empire was to be preserved, such recalcitrant and dangerous groups had to be destroyed. A decree issued by Decius required Christians and those suspected of Christian sympathies to prove their loyalty by the performance, in the presence of witnesses, of acts of sacrifice to the gods of the state. From Egypt have come several examples of affidavits signed by those who had conformed with the edict and certified by their witnesses. The Christians suffered grievously, but the church survived and even gained strength from its ordeal. The last great persecution was ordered by Diocletian, who sought to force the church to yield to the autocratic state as all other individuals and institutions had been compelled to do. Christians were excluded from the privileges of citizenship, many heads of the church were arrested, and church property was confiscated or destroyed.

The Development of Christianity

Despite the handicap of opposition and persecution, the number of Christians increased, and by the opening of the fourth century they were to be found in all the provinces of the Empire. Persecution only made the Christians more conscious of their mission, more energetic and more aggressive in their proselytizing efforts. They often welcomed the crown of martyrdom in order to demonstrate their zeal for their faith and to attract new converts. Converts were now being made among the upper classes of society, including intellectuals, who began to produce an intensive literature of defense against anti-Christian acts and writings. In their efforts to dispel misrepresentations about their religion, these writers helped to set forth the nature of the Christian faith and to develop its doctrines.

Among the greatest of the theologians in the late second and early third centuries were Clement and Origen, both from Alexandria, who employed pagan learning in the service of the Christian faith as they strove to harmonize Christianity and Greek philosophy. Origen in particular explained the Bible and especially the story of Creation in terms of Plato's philosophy and its fundamental dualism of mind and matter. According to Origen the material world was created for the correction and education of fallen "intelligences" who would be redeemed by Christ. This process of fall and redemption would be repeated an infinite number of times until matter would finally be completely overcome by Christ. In the West during these early centuries, other apologists, the fiery Tertullian in the Severan period, the erudite Arnobius in the third century, and his pupil Lactantius, the "Christian Cicero," defended the faith with eloquence and learning.

Growth of the Christian Hierarchy

The organization of the church was strengthened during this period, and Christians developed a proud self-consciousness that they belonged to a universal body. The small, independent communities which had made up the primitive church were being replaced by an ecclesiastical hierarchy modeled upon the Roman system of provincial administration. Originally administrative and religious functions had been performed by deacons, presbyters or elders, and bishops or overseers, all of whom were elected by the members of the congregations to which they belonged. Now the clergy was clearly differentiated from laymen, who ceased to participate actively in the administration of their church communities. More and more power was concentrated in the hands of the bishops, to whose authority the presbyters, now priests, were subject. The separate communities were brought together on a provincial or wider basis, and the bishops from the capitals of the Roman provinces gained the leadership in these larger units.

The Triumph of Christianity

Slowly and painfully, in the face of obstacles and opposition, Christianity was winning its way in the Roman world. Handicapped as no other religion was by the hostility of the government, Christianity nevertheless continued to make fresh converts on every level of society and everywhere in the Empire. Less than a generation after the great persecutions by Diocletian, the Roman emperor Constantine accepted Christianity as his own religion, and three-quarters of a century later the pagan cults were proscribed and banned, as Christianity had once been. What caused this remarkable reversal in the fortunes of the Christian church?

Those external factors which had fostered the spread of the Oriental mystery religions favored Christianity as well: the unity of the Roman world, the ease of communications, hard times from which men sought relief or escape. Like the eastern cults, Christianity offered a solution for many problems and gave assurance of salvation from sin and evil in a life to come. The spiritual appeal of Christianity was, however, apparently greater than that of any other religion from the East. It made no distinction between rich and poor, freeman and slave, male and female. Its ethical teachings were lofty: "Whatsoever ye would that men should do unto you, even so do unto them." It preached charity and brotherly love: "He that loveth not his brother whom he hath seen, how can he love God whom he hath not seen?"

Its theology was clear-cut and intelligible. That in certain respects, for example, in its discussion of heaven and hell and of a last judgment, it had analogies with other contemporary religions was an advantage, since it posed these problems in terms familiar to devotees of these religions. The Christian teachings were clearly stated in the Old and the New Testament, and in time learned Christians both in the Greek East and the Latin West helped to develop the doctrines of the church. Beginning with Paul, effective missionaries spread the message of Christianity to the Roman world. Their task was facilitated because, unlike the Oriental cults, none of which had a central organization, Christianity was a universal religion whose separate communities were in close communication with each other. It was not long before these separate churches were drawn together into a tightly knit organization under the control of a disciplined body of administrative and religious officials. This too was a powerful asset to Christianity. Moreover, men were prepared to die for their faith. "The blood of the martyrs the seed of the church," is more than a vivid phrase. It describes the zeal and enthusiasm which Christianity inspired in its followers. For every Christian martyr the church gained hundreds of converts, many of whom were impressed by the heroism of those who chose death rather than a denial of their religion. Most important of all the factors which attracted men to Christianity was the appeal of an historic founder who had appeared not in a remote past, but in recent times and in the Roman Empire.

The Christian Roman Empire

In 313, by the so-called Edict of Milan, the emperor Constantine and his colleague Licinius granted toleration to the

Christians and gave their religion equal status with others. A few years later Constantine himself became a Christian. Whether this action was dictated, as some historians have held, by motives of political expediency, or whether, as seems more probable, it stemmed from religious conviction and conversion, it helped to assure the victory of Christianity. The emperor did not make Christianity the religion of the state nor did he ban other religions, but his zeal for Christianity was intense. As he strove valiantly to maintain a unified church in a united state, he extended special privileges to the religion which he himself had accepted. When Constantine died in 337, the Empire was clearly Christian, and this was emphasized a few years later when the official ceremonies in honor of the pagan gods were abolished. To be sure, the emperor Julian (361–363) made a futile effort to restore paganism by creating a universal pagan creed on the Christian model. His last words, "Pale Galilean, thou hast conquered," may be apocryphal, but they epitomize the actual state of affairs. Within a few years Christianity had become the official religion of Rome. The emperor Theodosius I (378–395) declared the pagan worship illegal, and as the state had once sought to destroy Christianity, so now it launched a bitter campaign to suppress paganism. In the course of a century a persecuted religion had become not merely the official religion of the state, but the only legally recognized and privileged religion in the Roman Empire.

The peril from the state was thus finally overcome, but victory posed many knotty problems for the church: how to deal with sectarian strife within the church; what was to be accepted as orthodox belief; what kind of life was the truly Christian; how to create an administrative machine adequate for an expanding organization with temporal as well as spiritual concerns? We shall describe later some of the solutions which the church found for these problems.

Christianity became the dominant religion of the western world and transformed its civilization in many ways. If Christianity was not, as Gibbon believed it was, one of the major causes of the decline of the Roman Empire, its victory signified the decline of ancient civilization. When the Empire passed away, the church succeeded and superseded it. Upon the foundation of the triumphant Christian religion the new world of the Middle Ages was slowly erected.

CHAPTER IV

Decline and Fall ~~~~~~~~~~~

FROM St. Augustine (354–430), in whose lifetime Italy and Rome were overrun by barbarian invaders, to the present, historians, philosophers, and theologians have sought an answer to one of the central problems of history: what caused the decline of the Roman Empire? What were the forces of dissolution? What were the weaknesses in the Roman Empire? What, in the words of the great eighteenth-century historian Edward Gibbon, were "the most important circumstances of its decline and fall: a revolution which will ever be remembered, and is still felt by the nations of the Earth?"

For each generation the question has had a topical as well as a historical interest. Consciously or not, men have sensed in that decline a foreshadowing of the fate of their own civilization and have tried, by seeking the causes of Rome's decline, to escape the same misfortune. Their own basic assumptions about the meaning of history, their own philosophy of history, have inevitably dictated the answers which men have given to the question.

Historical Explanations of the Decline

To Ammianus Marcellinus (born c.330), the last great Roman historian, a decline in personal morality was the

cause of the ills which afflicted the Empire. The more profound mind of St. Augustine saw in the calamities of his
day one act in the great unfolding drama of universal history. In *The City of God* (*De Civitate Dei*), a work which
for more than a thousand years continued to mold the mind
of mediaeval man, Augustine looked beyond the somber
present, beyond Rome, beyond the transitory city of the
world, to the eternal City of God. The earthly city of Rome
was passing, not because of the abandonment of the pagan
gods for Christianity, as some critics charged, but as the necessary and fortunate preparation for the triumph of the
heavenly city where man's destiny was to be attained. The
events of Rome's history, therefore, were unrolling as part
of the general plan of the universe.

In contrast to this interpretation based upon the Christian
faith stands Gibbon's explanation, which was rooted in
eighteenth-century rationalist thought. The historian saw
the decline not as the preparation for something better, but
as a tragedy which he sums up in the sentence: "I have
described the triumph of Barbarism and Religion."

In our own times there has been an equally wide range of
explanations, each reflecting the crises of the twentieth
century: Spengler's belief, expounded in *The Decline of
the West*, that history, Egyptian or Roman, follows a
predetermined course from birth to childhood and from
maturity to old age and death; Rostovtzeff's thesis of the
failure of ancient civilization to reach the masses and the re-
sulting conflict between the educated, propertied urban
classes and the ignorant and impoverished rural masses to
whose level culture declined; and most recently Toynbee's
view that a symptom of decay is the failure of a civilization
to assimilate its "internal proletariat," those who have no

real stake in society, or its "external proletariat," the barbarians on the frontiers.

Confronted with much the same data about the decline of the Empire, writers have offered widely varying interpretations of their meaning. The problem, therefore, is one of abiding interest, as much for what it reveals about historians and their times as for the light it sheds upon history. No more than others can we presume to offer a definite solution to the riddle, but we must at least present the question and analyze some possible answers.

Problems in Evaluating the Decline

The decline of the Roman Empire was neither sudden nor cataclysmic, but was a gradual process extending over several centuries. We have already examined many of the disquieting symptoms of decay and disintegration which appeared during the third and even the second century A.D., and we have seen how successive emperors applied force and compulsion in order to maintain the integrity of the Empire. Important as their achievement was, Diocletian and Constantine succeeded only in postponing the collapse of the Roman Empire, not in preventing it. After the death of Constantine in 337, the signs of decay increased, and the world of the fifth and sixth centuries, while it preserved many elements of ancient civilization, was already recognizably mediaeval. On the soil of the western half of the Roman Empire, Germanic kingdoms were established; while in the East, Byzantine emperors ruled as heirs to the Romans. Trade continued, but on a diminishing scale, and agriculture was increasingly on the basis of large, self-sufficient estates worked by serfs who were bound to the soil. The pagan cults yielded to Christianity, the Christian church built a strongly centralized administrative system, and classical learning was adapted to Christian needs or was superseded by Christian theology.

Roman armies had been defeated by Germanic invaders before, but the catastrophic defeat of the Romans in 378 at the battle of Adrianople, which will be treated later, was a dramatic proof that the imperial government was unable to offer effective resistance to invasion. This was underscored in 410, when the barbarians occupied and sacked Rome. Finally in 476 Romulus Augustulus, the last Roman emperor in the West, lost his throne and soon the invaders gained full control of the western half of the Roman Empire. The Empire had experienced other crises in the past and had surmounted them; now it was unable to rally. A government which for centuries had united almost the whole civilized world into one empire was disintegrating. Meanwhile the acceptance of Christianity by the emperors and the vast majority of their subjects was both cause and effect of a profound transformation in the civilization of the ancient world. To this theme Gibbon gave a title which has become traditional: *The Decline and Fall of the Roman Empire.* Closer study has revealed that Gibbon exaggerated the extent of decline: there were elements of vitality as well as signs of decay in the centuries after the Antonine Age. Some historians, indeed, have insisted that there was no real decline, but merely a transformation of civilization. Nevertheless, if from whatever point of view—political, economic, or cultural—we compare the Roman world of the third and fourth centuries with the Empire during the first two centuries, we find indisputable evidences of decline.

Whether we designate what occurred as change or decline, we are concerned with a very complex phenomenon.

Many of the explanations have been oversimplified solutions to an immensely difficult problem. Scholars have sometimes selected one factor, for example, the barbarian invasions or the exhaustion of the soil, and have declared it to be the ultimate cause of the decline of the Roman Empire, or they have looked for one common denominator of decline to which they have reduced all other factors. We shall see, however, that the process of decline was due not to a single cause, but to a variety of interacting factors—political, economic, social, cultural, and psychological. To give priority to any one of them is virtually impossible, since each acted with and upon every other factor. At the outset, therefore, we should recognize the principle of multiple causation.

The Distinction between Causes and Symptoms

A more common error arises out of the difficulty of distinguishing between cause and symptom. Many of the alleged causes are actually symptoms of decline due to antecedent causes or conditions, rather than ultimate causes in themselves. Some of the symptoms of decay are obvious: economic collapse, inadequate revenues, insufficient armed forces to defend the Empire, intellectual stagnation. Each of these factors, however, is itself in need of explanation. Each is a symptom of decline and at the same time a cause of further decline, in other words, an effect of an antecedent cause and a cause itself.

An example or two may illustrate the difficulty of differentiating between cause and symptom and between proximate and remote causes. We have seen how Romans or Romanized elements, those who had the largest stake in Roman institutions, came to form a dwindling minority in the army. The barbarization of the army and the civil service and Rome's dependence upon barbarian allies and mercenaries were undoubtedly one of the factors in the decline of Rome. But more and more Germans were admitted into the army and the civil service because Rome desperately needed men to help defend her frontiers and administer her empire. The barbarization of the Empire is, therefore, a symptom of decay, an indication that there was a shortage of manpower in relation to the tasks which had to be performed. What caused that? Was it a declining birth rate, high mortality in wars and epidemics, or increased requirements for men? Each and all may have been remote causes of the barbarization of the Empire, and the process of barbarization was itself both symptom and cause of decline.

Again, the insistent needs of the army and the bureaucracy imposed an enormous burden upon the treasury. The high cost of continuous warfare, the shrinking revenues which followed the loss of provinces, the dislocation of trade as a result of civil war, the depreciation of the coinage —all these had a ruinous effect upon the economic life of the Empire. The methods devised by the imperial government to meet soaring expenses reduced men to the level of slaves of the state, straining to support a costly machinery of defense and administration. Individual and municipal freedom was destroyed by the central government, and with the loss of that freedom initiative and enterprise were paralyzed. Was this a cause of decline? Or did the imperial government adopt the Draconian solution of binding merchants and artisans to their callings, farmers to the land, and city officials to their posts because the emperors believed that only by mobilizing all their resources in this way could they save the Empire? Again we have symptoms of decline which are at the same time causes springing from other causes, each interacting upon the other, each an aspect of the whole causative process. Moreover, some factors, whether they are regarded as causes or symptoms, cannot be measured accurately. By tracing the deterioration of the coinage, we may describe with some precision such physical phenomena as the shrinking supply of precious metal, but we have no yardstick for measuring other aspects of the decline of the Empire, such as apathy or "loss of nerve." We can only infer that they existed both as causes and as symptoms of decline.

Some Unfounded Theories of the Decline

Some alleged causes may be rejected at once. Thus a major climatic change, an increasing drought caused by the diminution of rainfall, has been held responsible for the decline of ancient civilization. Long spells of dry weather are said to have led to the exhaustion of the soil, poor crops, abandonment of the land, impoverishment, famine, and depopulation. This remains, however, a hypothesis for which no valid evidence from the whole Empire has been adduced. A closely related physical factor, the exhaustion of the soil, has also been suggested. In certain districts, for example, in southern Italy, deforestation and other factors undoubtedly reduced the fertility of the soil, but there is no evidence for a general exhaustion of the soil throughout the Empire, despite primitive methods of fertilizing and farming. On the contrary, Gaul continued to produce bountiful crops in the late Roman Empire, and Egypt, largely dependent upon the flood waters of the Nile, had its fertility renewed annually.

Some scholars have explained the decline of Rome on the

basis of biological factors. There are no scientifically acceptable data to support the argument that societies, like individuals, have a life-cycle—birth, growth, maturity, and death—and hence that civilizations like individuals are predestined to die. Nor can we accept the hypothesis that the "best" elements in Roman society were exterminated by wars and revolution or died out because of the disinclination of these members of society to reproduce. We are given neither a satisfactory definition of the "best," nor proof that only the "best" perished. Similarly, one may dispose of the related argument that Rome succumbed because of "race suicide" or "race mixture," that is, that the "superior Roman stock" was overwhelmed by "inferior races" who bred freely while the "best" failed to reproduce. Biologists and anthropologists have demonstrated that there are no superior or inferior races. The decline of Rome has also been attributed to malaria or to the great plague which occurred in the reign of Marcus Aurelius, but malaria was not endemic throughout the Empire, and the effects of the plague, however deadly, might have been overcome were it not for other factors which we shall analyze later. In any event, we cannot be sure that Rome would have been saved by a larger population.

Moralists have suggested that the decline was caused by a slackening of personal morality, but most of the evidence they have presented is from the flourishing years of the early Principate. In the Later Empire, under the influence of the religious revival, morals may actually have been elevated. In any case, most people in both the earlier and the later period seem to have lived decent and sober lives. Even if moral standards had decayed, it would still be necessary to seek an explanation for such an historical phenomenon.

The Role of Social Conflict

The decline of ancient civilization has been attributed, by Rostovtzeff, to the failure of the upper classes to extend their culture to the rural and urban lower classes.[1] In the end, according to this argument, there was a prolonged social conflict between the urban propertied classes and the rural masses who made up the bulk of the army. The masses put their leaders on the throne, absorbed the higher classes, and lowered standards in general. But there is little evidence that the army was made up of a class-conscious proletariat which hated the urban upper classes. On the contrary, in its greed the army plundered town and country alike. Yet so much of the argument must be granted: that Roman culture had not penetrated sufficiently into the masses, had not inspired them with devotion to a high ideal to which all alike were committed, and that now in a time of mounting difficulties it failed to evoke their active effort and co-operation in its defense.

Another unsatisfactory hypothesis is that the lack of any clear constitutional provision for the succession on the death of an emperor led to military usurpation of power, anarchy, and all its concomitant evils. The method of adoption of an heir to the throne by the incumbent, haphazard as it may have been, worked well during most of the Antonine period. Indeed, the choice of the ablest man available, regardless of family affiliation, worked better than Marcus Aurelius' solution of designating his own son Commodus as emperor.

Finally, the Empire was not suddenly destroyed by the barbarians, although their attack contributed to Rome's

[1] Rostovtzeff, *op. cit.*

decline and eventually they took possession of the western half of the Roman Empire. The pressure of barbarians had been felt by the Romans from very early times, and the invasions of the fifth century were not much more formidable than previous ones which had been repelled. If Rome had not already been weakened internally and demoralized, she might have put up an effective resistance, as she had to earlier onslaughts.

Political Factors

We have rejected certain explanations of the decline of ancient civilization. What factors remain? Among the political factors may be counted the failure of the civil power to control the army. We have seen how the troops were preoccupied with making and unmaking emperors and how ambitious generals fought for the throne. The result was military disorganization, which facilitated the advance of the barbarians. We have observed both as a symptom and as a cause of decline the decay of civic vitality, as the emperors interfered more and more with municipal freedom and thus undermined a civilization which had been based upon an association of self-governing city-states. The municipal aristocracy, the backbone of that civilization, was crushed by a harsh and arbitrary despotism and old loyalties were weakened. Cities decayed and eventually many of them disappeared.

What lay behind these changes? It has been suggested that Rome acquired a larger empire than she could control effectively, that imperialism was the basic fault from which stemmed all other weaknesses: an insubordinate army, a top-heavy bureaucracy, political corruption, oppression of individuals and cities, class warfare, the growth of slavery, the influx of alien ideas. The difficulties of defending and governing too large an empire, it has been said, were complicated by primitive methods of transportation and communication. Should the Romans have stopped at the borders fixed by Augustus (31 B.C.–A.D. 14), or at the borders of 133 B.C., or 272 B.C., or 509 B.C.? Each acquisition of territory obviously posed fresh problems, but it was a measure of Rome's greatness that for centuries she solved many of these problems, and a measure of her decline that ultimately she was unable to do so. We must seek if we can some explanation for her failure other than the paradox that her rise caused her decline.

The End of Expansion

It may be argued, on the contrary, that a basic factor of decline was not overexpansion, but a cessation of expansion. Within the geographical limits set by the emperor Hadrian (117–138), Rome quickly attained the maximum possibilities of exploitation under existing techniques and economic stagnation set in. Since her wealth was no longer replenished by the plunder and resources of new provinces, there was a shift from an economy which had grown with the Empire to a static economy. Meanwhile pressures on the frontiers increased, and the government was compelled to maintain more armed forces and administrative officials than she could afford. Higher taxes, bureaucratic and autocratic controls, and the whole machinery of compulsion followed.

Further expansion, however, would have been neither feasible with the resources of manpower which Rome had available nor immediately profitable. As an alternative the Romans might have extended their domestic markets. But the purchasing power of the mass of the people was always limited, and the requirements of the rich were not sufficient to compensate for the limited demands of the majority of men. It has been suggested that an abundance of cheap slave labor prevented the invention and use of labor-saving machinery which might have produced cheap products and thus stimulated the economy by extending the internal market. Long before the fourth century, however, with the cessation of expansion, slaves were neither readily available nor cheap and there was, in fact, a labor shortage. A more valid explanation of the failure to produce a machine technology was the inability of the impoverished masses to purchase its products. The civil and foreign wars of the third century further dislocated the limited markets, and the economic structure of the Empire was badly shaken. The very measures taken by the government to preserve the Empire weakened and finally paralyzed initiative and enterprise.

The Disintegration of Central Authority

We have traced the growth of an inefficient and oppressive financial system which was both cause and result of economic decline. We have seen how the normal requirements of defense and administration and the extraordinary costs of half a century of military anarchy led to higher taxes, depreciation of the coinage, extension of the system of compulsory requisitions and forced labor, and economic chaos. The enforcement of the system called for an ever larger and more elaborate machinery of government and more repressive measures. As men sought to escape the insatiable demands of the state, they were regimented and bound to their classes and callings. The heavy hand of a centralized bureaucracy lay upon everyone, but especially upon the townsfolk. Men lost public spirit as well as individual initiative, and the failure of both was a portent of the decline of ancient civilization. These are some of the aspects of decline, but it must be remembered that in taking these measures the emperors were trying to prop up a structure which was already tottering and that these measures were therefore symptoms as well as causes of decline.

Economic decentralization was another factor. The provincials either had their own industrial skills or quickly developed them. Soon they began to manufacture goods themselves for local and even for imperial markets, and the market for Roman and Italian products shrank as competition from new provincial industries increased. Although the Empire was linked by an excellent system of roads and seaways, the methods of transportation were relatively poor. The normal difficulties of movement from one region to another were intensified by the disorders of a century of crisis. Thus high costs and risks helped promote economic decentralization, and provincial autarchy in turn fostered political disintegration.

Related to these economic and political developments was the growth of large estates cultivated by slaves and semiservile *coloni*. The free peasantry, once a major element in the strength of the Roman Empire, sank to the status of dependents. As early as the time of the Gracchi (133–121 B.C.) this evil had been apparent; now the whole process was intensified. In the end it led to the development of more or less self-sufficient large estates which in turn advanced economic decentralization.

Intellectual and Psychological Aspects of Decline

It is extremely difficult to assess the intellectual and psychological aspects of decline, but certain characteristics may be noted. Gibbon and others considered Christianity a major cause of the decline of ancient civilization. To be sure, the Christian attitude of resignation to adversity and the Christian emphasis upon a life to come represented a surrender to the material difficulties which beset men rather than a struggle to overcome them. But this is only a phase of the changing intellectual interests of the ancient world. As a result of the chaos and dislocation of life, there was a growing note of pessimism and despair which led to apathy and inertia. A reflection of this was the shift of interest from the here to the hereafter. We have seen how, under the stress of political, economic, and social ills, men turned to other-worldly religions, the Oriental mystery cults and Christianity. As they lost confidence in the Empire and in their own power to alter conditions, they tried to find inner security as compensation for a world which was grim and uncertain. This groping for salvation in new religions is one aspect of the psychological change; another is the resignation to the misfortunes of this world: to a totalitarian regime, a collapsing economy, and the barbarian invaders themselves. There was a "loss of nerve," as it has been called, a breakdown of morale, a defeatist mentality. Even if they had the means, men no longer had the will to maintain the Empire against invasion and dissolution. An intellectual collapse accompanied and hastened the decline of the Roman Empire.

In the final analysis, it was interaction of many factors, some hidden, some only partly discerned, some obvious, which resulted in the decline of ancient civilization. A nexus of political, social, economic, and psychological factors, each both cause and symptom of decline, accounts for the phenomenon. In time we may have more evidence and other historical methods which may enable us to determine with a greater degree of precision and accuracy the causes of historical events. Meanwhile we may study the facts and seek to establish their meaning, but we cannot always say categorically and definitely how and why great historical phenomena, like the decline of Rome, occurred.

Our description of the maladies which beset Rome must not make us think that all was unrelieved gloom. The foundations of Roman civilization endured and on them mediaeval civilization was built. In the West the Germanic kingdoms inherited many elements of Roman civilization; while in the Byzantine East, ancient civilization, adapted to Christian purposes, flourished for a thousand years. Both in the East and West the Christian church assumed many of the functions of Rome. In the period of transition which we shall now consider much was preserved and much was salvaged from the ruin of the ancient world. A continuous thread linked the old and the new, and out of the chaos and confusion the mediaeval world slowly emerged.

CHAPTER V

Europe in Transition

THE fourth to the seventh centuries mark the decline of the ancient world and the birth of the mediaeval. At the beginning of this age of transition the Roman Empire, though shaken by the crises of the third century, still stood firm and fast. At the end of the period a shattered and broken world was beginning a slow and painful process of reconstruction. During these centuries the western half of the Empire was lost to the Germanic invaders, who succeeded in establishing kingdoms of their own on its soil. From their capital at Constantinople the Eastern Roman emperors defended their realm from invasion and created a power which was strong enough under the emperor Justinian (527–565) to challenge the Germanic states of the West and to recapture from them part of the lost Roman territory. Enormously strengthened by Constantine's conversion, Christianity consolidated its victory over paganism, became first the dominant and then the only legal religion of the Empire, and in time won over the barbarians. Among its followers the church created a firmer discipline by defining its doctrines more precisely and by building an efficient administrative organization. The development of monasticism strengthened the church at a

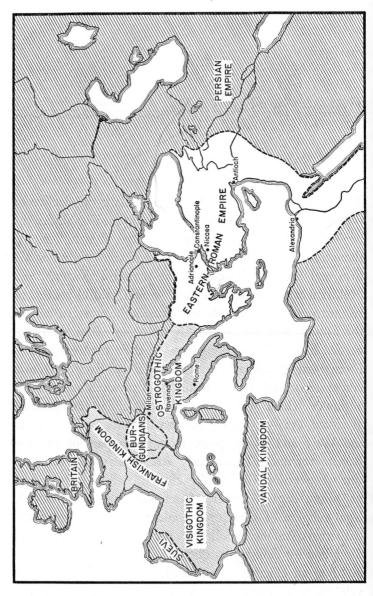

time when its energies were being consumed in resisting the growth of heretical movements. The hostility which Christian writers and thinkers manifested toward classical culture as something rooted in the detested paganism slowly abated as the pagan gods themselves disappeared. Through Christianity the heritage of classical culture was transmitted to the mediaeval world.

The Empire Restored

Constantine the Great had been hailed in an imperial edict as "restorer of the human race, extender of the Empire and of Roman dominion, founder of everlasting security." With his predecessor Diocletian he had staved off the disintegration of the Empire and had given it a stability which it had not known for at least three-quarters of a century. An army of functionaries now administered the state more efficiently and more ruthlessly, and Rome's soldiers ably resisted Persians and Germans. Yet order and security were short-lived, and when Constantine died in 337, Roman history unrolled once more against that dark background of tension and turbulence which had characterized the third century. The defenses against the Germans and Persians were permitted to crumble while rival aspirants fought each other for the throne. For many Romans, apathy about the present crisis, a nostalgia for the golden past, or a preoccupation with a future located not in pagan Rome but in the heavenly city of the Christian church took the place of confidence in the Empire's power.

Scarcely had Constantine been laid to rest when civil war broke out among his heirs. For sixteen years the Empire was distracted by their feuds, until finally one of his sons, Constantius, succeeded in defeating his rivals and gaining sole rule for himself (353–361). But his power was threatened by rebellion and the familiar menace of barbarians and Persians. His successor Julian died fighting on the Persian front in 363, and within a year the Empire was divided between an eastern and a western ruler.

Strong governments had long held in check the centrifugal pull of cultural differences between East and West. With the progressive weakening of the imperial regime, however, these differences became an important factor in the division of the Empire, which was undertaken voluntarily by some emperors for reasons of policy or was forced upon others by their rivals. Thus in the fourth century the ultimate split between a Western and an Eastern Roman Empire was foreshadowed. Nevertheless, in theory the Empire remained united, and it was the ambition of the more energetic and aggressive rulers to translate into reality the ideal of a single state.

The Battle of Adrianople

Throughout the fourth and fifth centuries the emperors fought desperately to protect their realms from the advancing waves of barbarians. The Eastern Empire escaped the worst ravages, but the Western Empire, less fortunately situated, was finally destroyed. For at least two centuries Rome had fought the barbarians on the Rhine-Danube frontier and more recently in far-off Britain, but the real beginning of the Germanic invasions occurred in 378, when two-thirds of the Roman army of the East, the ablest generals, and the emperor Valens himself were destroyed by the Visigoths in the battle of Adrianople.

"Only night put an end to this irreparable disaster, the consequences of which will long weigh upon the destinies of the Empire." So wrote the Roman historian Ammianus Marcellinus, who terminated his account of Roman history with this battle. He found its only parallel in Greek and Roman history to be the battle of Cannae, the terrible defeat which the Romans suffered in the war against Hannibal six centuries earlier. And Ammianus' judgment has been accepted by Gibbon and other historians, who see in Adrianople a turning-point in history, a watershed between the ancient and mediaeval worlds. The battle did more than expose the weakness of Rome to the barbarians and encourage them to return to the attack again and again, for never afterward did they leave Roman soil. Adrianople marks also a revolution in the history of warfare. The infantry upon which Rome had primarily depended for centuries and with which she had conquered the Mediterranean world had proved no match for the Gothic cavalry in this battle. Henceforth for many centuries cavalry units, whether German or Roman—for in time the Romans learned the lesson—were to play a major role in warfare. In military tactics, too, the Middle Ages were foreshadowed in the declining Empire.

Theodosius the Great

Only with difficulty did Theodosius the Great (378–395), on his succession to the throne, rebuild an army and force a peace upon the plundering hordes. But as the price of peace the Visigoths and their kinsmen, the Ostrogoths, were settled on abandoned lands within the Empire as self-governing allies (*foederati*) with an obligation to furnish troops for the Roman army in return for fixed subsidies. Clearly the Germanic tribal chieftains' taking an oath of loyalty to the emperor and the payment of troops in land anticipated the feudal relationships of the Middle Ages. Fraught with more consequence for the moment was the establishment of a mass of Germans, a compact nation in effect within the Roman state. No longer was the Danube a safe frontier, and within a century the barbarians occupied the territories of the Western Empire.

In 394 Theodosius brought the whole Roman Empire under his control. An able administrator, a distinguished general, and a doughty champion of Christianity, Rome's last great emperor strove valiantly to preserve the Empire, but the old evils remained unchecked and even multiplied. The remedies for Rome's ills which Constantine had employed to advantage at the beginning of the century were no longer efficacious, and Theodosius' successes proved ephemeral. With his death in 395 the Roman Empire was permanently divided into Eastern and Western Empires. Whatever the devices employed thereafter to preserve the fiction of imperial unity, the Empire was clearly partitioned into two independent states by the end of the fourth century.

The Rule of the Generals

The majority of Theodosius' successors in the West ruled in name only, for the effective power now belonged to the generals, whose armies consisted largely of men who, like themselves, were of barbarian origin. Dangerous as the practice was of entrusting the safety of Rome to barbarians, the emperors seemed unable to find another solution. Hard pressed by the invaders, they needed soldiers and they recruited them among the very people they were trying to keep out of the Empire. The loyalty of these troops was at best dubious. The soldiers followed their generals and the generals were often more concerned with wielding political power than in defending an empire to which neither they nor their men were attached by tradition or sentiment. Indeed, barbarian chieftains—the Visigoth Alaric is a striking example—fought Rome on occasion in an effort to wrest from the emperor a high military office; so strong still was the prestige of Rome, so greatly did the barbarians covet Roman titles and powers.

Some German generals, to be sure, fought valiantly and faithfully against the invaders: Stilicho the Vandal, at the beginning of the fifth century, was a tower of strength against the Visigoths, and half a century later the Sueve Ricimer defended Rome against the Vandals. But their military power tempted them to make and unmake emperors, and Rome suffered as she had in the disastrous third and fourth centuries from internecine rivalries and wars, intrigues and conspiracies, Romans against barbarian invaders, barbarians against other barbarians, German generals against Roman administrators, generals against emperors, East against West. Small wonder then that the barbarians were able to cross the frontiers and to range almost unchecked deep within the Western Empire.

The Sack of Rome

In 410 Visigothic invaders marched through the streets of Rome, which had remained inviolate in the eight hundred years since the Gauls had sacked the city. Under the leadership of Alaric, their first king—who had won his rank in the decade or so after Adrianople, had simultaneously held high military office under the Romans, had fought for Rome, and fought and intrigued against her—the Visigoths moved into the heart of the Italian peninsula, took Rome by siege, and pillaged the great city. Although Ravenna in northeastern Italy had become the capital of the Western Empire in 404, the magic of Rome's name was undiminished and Romans everywhere were shocked by the reports of the calamity. Far away in Bethlehem, St. Jerome lamented when he heard the news from refugees: "The lamp of the world is extinguished, and it is the whole world which has perished in the ruins of this one city." [1] In Africa, St. Augustine wrote his greatest work, *The City of God*, to explain the disaster and to refute the charge that a city which had triumphed over its enemies as long as the pagan gods were worshiped had succumbed at last because its rulers had accepted Christianity. The Goths withdrew from Rome as quickly as they had come, but in 455 Rome was once more sacked by barbarians, this time by the Vandals from Africa.

The End of the Western Empire

The whole West was in utter chaos. The frontier provinces were lost; Picts, Scots, and Saxons overran Britain, from which Roman troops had been withdrawn around 400; Gaul swarmed with Franks, Burgundians and Alemanni, Huns, Visigoths, and Vandals; Spain with Suevi, Vandals, and Visigoths; Africa with Vandals. This was the grim situation which St. Jerome described early in the century; it became worse as the century advanced: "Time has dried our tears, and save for a few old men, the rest, born in captivity and siege, no longer regret the liberty of which the very memory is lost. But who could believe that Rome on her own soil fights no longer for her glory, but for her existence, and no longer even fights, but purchases her life with gold and precious things?" [2]

[1] Jerome, *Commentary on Ezekiel*, I, Prologue.
[2] Jerome, *Letters*, CXXIII, 17.

Thus the Western Empire fell apart, and by the end of the century all the provinces and Italy itself were ruled by German kings. In 476 barbarian mercenaries deposed the last Western Roman emperor, a boy whose name, Romulus Augustulus, by a strange irony recalled the founder of Rome and the founder of the Empire. In his place they elevated Odoacer, a fellow German. This episode marks the formal end of the Western Roman Empire, although barbarian leaders had for years exercised effective power there. But even after 476 the fiction of imperial rule was maintained. With the disappearance of the Roman emperor of the West, the Eastern emperor claimed to be the source of authority, and his overlordship was recognized at least nominally by the new Germanic kings of the West who sought to gain from Constantinople acquiescence in their rule. In the eyes of their Roman subjects they thereby acquired a measure of legitimacy and shared the prestige which still attached to the name of the Roman Empire.

For nearly three hundred years the Romans had suffered from civil war and disorder, economic distress, a lowering of moral standards, a sense of futility—in short, all the symptoms of decay which have been analyzed in earlier chapters. The last century of the Western Empire only accentuated these evils. True, for some contemporaries Rome still seemed to shine with undimmed luster. In her darkest hour pagan and even Christian writers extolled the grandeur and the glory of Rome and her historic mission of uniting mankind under the Roman peace. Yet the weight of other evidence makes clear the desperate plight of Rome's subjects long before they were overwhelmed by the barbarians.

The old evils and abuses remained and new ones appeared. The emergency legislation of Diocletian and Constantine was made permanent as the crisis continued and indeed worsened because of the very remedies employed. The army, made up now largely of barbarians, continued to play a sinister role in politics, while from behind the throne the generals dictated the policies of many of the emperors. An already swollen, wasteful, and corrupt bureaucracy was expanded in order to provide enough officials to keep men in the hereditary classes and occupations to which they were bound. Thus the state tried to secure the labor and the money needed to support the complicated structure of defense and administration. For most Romans there was scant hope of escape from their crushing responsibilities, from what an imperial decree described as "the inexorable compulsion of the laws by which everybody is bound to submit his own fortune without exemptions due to office or privilege, in order that the public interest may not suffer any injury or loss, and to render such bodily service as his father's or ancestor's status or his own may require." [3] Flight to other classes and other occupations, to the army, the civil service, the church, to the wilderness or the desert, all these loopholes were blocked by imperial legislation. Hope and enterprise vanished, despair and apathy took their place. There was little incentive or will to resist the barbarian invaders.

Beginnings of Feudalism and the Manorial System

However desperate the plight of large segments of the population, some individuals and classes enjoyed power, prestige, and prosperity. We have seen that the generals who had effective control of the Empire were a familiar

[3] *Codex Justinianus*, X, 71, 4.

part of the scene in the fourth and fifth centuries. Many of them were of German origin and all of them depended upon barbarian troops bound to them by ties of personal loyalty. These army commanders, who resembled feudal lords of the Middle Ages, were a potent force in the Later Roman Empire.

Exempt, too, from the general decline were the landed aristocrats who lived on their great estates as virtual rulers. The weakness of the emperors and the disorders arising from civil war and invasion enabled them to acquire enormous power. They built their estates through imperial gifts, by forcible confiscation and seizure, by taking over waste land and abandoned farms, and by offering protection to small farmers in return for land. Powerful enough to escape the payment of taxes and to evade municipal responsibilities, they became, in effect, feudal lords with financial and judicial control over their tenants and occasionally with private armies of their own. Despite the opposition of the central government, whose fears were aroused by the growing independence of these landed aristocrats, they continued to increase their vast holdings. Their fortified villas, forerunners of mediaeval manors, were like islands of security and prosperity in the turbulent fourth and fifth centuries.

Most men were much less fortunate than the relative handful of generals and landlords. The class of small independent landowners whose decline had been steady now virtually disappeared. Those who survived earlier vicissitudes voluntarily turned over their farms to wealthier landlords who could provide protection against barbarians or relief from grasping tax collectors. They relinquished their freedom of movement and were bound permanently to the soil, which they now worked as tenant farmers or *coloni*. The land which they surrendered they received in the form of a *precarium*, that is, they enjoyed its use during their own lifetime and their children might in turn cultivate the land under the same arrangement. Meanwhile, in return for their services, landless farmers gained the protection of landlords, and under the name of *patrocinium* the old Republican system of client and patron was revived in an extreme form. Thus a long step was taken toward the mediaeval institution of serfdom. But while some farmers at least achieved a measure of security in this way, others, uprooted and desperate, formed themselves into bands of outlaws who waged war against the landlords and the government and even gave help to the barbarians.

Decline of Trade and the Urban Middle Class

The decline of the urban middle class, accelerated by the crises of the third century and the remedies prescribed by the emperors, gained momentum. The burden of municipal office-holding which its members had long been forced to assume was crushing, and by the fourth century the imperial autocracy closed nearly every avenue of escape from this form of bondage. The middle class suffered also from the spread of large estates or villas which produced in their own workshops most of the necessities of life. Yet though trade declined sharply it did not cease. There were still manufactured goods and even natural products which villas could not make or produce themselves. There was still a flourishing trade in luxury goods from distant lands: silks, spices, jewels, incense, and ivory for those who could afford them or for the church, which required them.

While barter tended to supersede money as a means of

exchange, there was no complete reversion to a barter economy and money continued to circulate in the remaining channels of trade. Some taxes were now collected in goods and some imperial functionaries were similarly paid in kind. But the state still collected various revenues, made some payments in cash, and issued a sound gold and silver currency which circulated at least among the wealthy. During the fourth century, moreover, emperors distributed to their troops and supporters quantities of gold and silver confiscated from pagan temples. The release of these stores of precious metals may have stimulated a depressed economy temporarily, but it also created inflationary prices and thus accelerated the decline.

At the end of the fourth century the situation of the middle class deteriorated sharply. Seaborne commerce suffered from the raids of Vandal pirates from North Africa and overland trade through the abandonment of Roman roads and the chaos caused by barbarian invasions. Most important, however, was the policy of the imperial government which, as the law codes show, overburdened the urban middle class and in the end destroyed that class and the industry and commerce which its members had fostered. It is one of the ironies of the history of the age that the emperors were forced to appoint in various cities special officials, the so-called defenders of the city, to keep the demands of their own tax collectors within bounds.

The decline of trade and manufacturing entailed the economic ruin of the cities which had been flourishing centers of Roman life in the West. As their populations shrank, the towns themselves contracted in area and became little more than centers for the transaction of imperial or ecclesiastical business. In the Later Empire, for example, in Gaul and Britain, new walls were built to enclose cities which had contracted to a quarter or less of their former size. Rome itself was no longer the proud and populous capital of a world empire, although it did acquire a new importance as the seat of the papacy. The barbarian invasions then completed the ruin of many of the western cities. Buildings became shabby and neglected, when they were not destroyed by wandering hordes; the poverty of the cities and of their inhabitants militated against the use of public and private funds for new construction. As the cults which they had served were outlawed, pagan temples fell into ruin or were converted into churches. Theaters and amphitheaters, public baths, aqueducts, all the amenities of Roman town life, decayed with the cities which they had served. Roman civilization had been essentially urban; mediaeval civilization was to be essentially rural. With the decline of the towns the general level of civilization was lowered and western Europe began to assume its mediaeval aspect.

Origins and Society of the Barbarians

We have seen that among the gravest of the problems confronting the Roman emperors from the time of Marcus Aurelius was the defense of the frontiers against barbarians. As Rome's powers of resistance weakened, the Germanic peoples pushed into the Empire, and on the territories of the western half which they helped to destroy they built their own kingdoms. Who were these wandering peoples? What were the consequences for European history of their victory over Rome? How much of the Roman institutional heritage did they accept and preserve?

For at least six hundred years before the German invaders

took possession of the lands of the Western Empire, the Romans had known them in peace and in war. Since the early Germanic peoples had no written literature of their own, we depend primarily upon Roman writers and archaeological evidence for our knowledge of them. We may supplement the information gleaned from these sources by drawing inferences from Germanic institutions and practices which survived into later times. In his *Commentaries on the Gallic Wars* (c.50 B.C.) Julius Caesar writes briefly about the character and the customs of the Germans, but our chief source is the *Germania*, a short and generally reliable essay written in A.D. 98 by the Roman historian Tacitus. From him we have a fascinating, if somewhat idealized, picture of the appearance of these tall, red-haired, blue-eyed Germans, their character, their warlike manner of life, and their primitive institutions.

Of their early history we know little. The original home of one group seems to have been in Scandinavia, while others dwelt along the shores of the Baltic between the Elbe and Oder Rivers. They lived or camped in rude huts which were grouped in small villages cleared out of primeval forest or set on ground high above surrounding marshlands. Seminomadic, pastoral peoples, they gained a livelihood by keeping herds and flocks, by hunting, and by raids on their neighbors. Rarely did they stay for many years in one place, but migrated from region to region in a search for food to maintain their expanding population. Gradually they spread out over a larger area. One group, made up of such tribes as the Franks, Alemanni, and Saxons, moved westward from the Baltic area and in time dispossessed the Celtic peoples of western and northern Germany. By about 200 B.C. they reached the Rhine, and a century later they

were established along the upper Danube and posed a
serious threat to Roman security. By his Gallic campaigns
in the 50's of the first century B.C. Caesar fixed the Rhine
as the Roman frontier, and the western Germans could
advance no farther. An increasing number of them had
turned meanwhile to a settled agricultural life and had
modified their institutions to meet the changing needs of
a farming folk. At the same time Roman merchants introduced them to the goods and the manners of the more
civilized Romans.

Between the sixth and the third centuries B.C. other German tribes whose original homes were in Scandinavia
crossed the Baltic and settled between the Oder and Vistula
Rivers. These East Germans, principally the Visigoths,
Ostrogoths, and Vandals, made their way gradually to the
south and east, to the lower Danube and the shores of the
Black Sea. They clung much longer than their western
kinsmen to the nomadic way of life and were still essentially
a pastoral folk in Tacitus' time, two centuries or so after
the West Germans had begun to adopt the more sedentary
habits of an agricultural people.

Among the Germanic peoples who abandoned their earlier nomadic ways society was divided into four classes:
nobles, freemen, serfs, and slaves. Birth and property determined nobility, and only nobles and freemen might own
land, but war and hunting were their usual occupations and
farming was left to those who were unable to fight: women,
old men, serfs, and slaves. Like the early Romans, the Germans had a strongly patriarchal society with the family
as the core. The family was held responsible for offenses
committed by one of its members. Murder, which was not
regarded as a capital crime, could be compensated by the

payment of a fine or *wergeld* to the family of the victim. Unless such satisfaction were made, however, all the members of the offending family were in danger of death by the blood feud. One of the most important elements in German society was the *comitatus*, a band of fighting companions bound by inviolate ties of personal loyalty to a chief who maintained them in return for their fighting services. From this institution, among others, mediaeval feudalism developed.

For purposes of military and political organization the village community formed the basic unit. Above the village was a hierarchy of larger territorial divisions: hundreds, counties, tribes, and, when kingship developed, kingdoms. The freemen in the village constituted the assembly, and in the hundreds and counties there were similar assemblies which met periodically in peacetime to consider civil affairs. In time of war or when mass migrations were undertaken, all the fighting men of the tribe or kingdom made up an assembly. Elected chiefs, marked out by qualities of leadership and courage, were originally at the head of the tribes, but by Tacitus' time the Germans had accepted hereditary kingship. As in other ancient communities, the role of the priests was also very important. They presided over the worship of deities who personified the forces of nature, practiced rites of divination, and helped to dispense a justice based upon a rudimentary law.

The Barbarian Invasions

For at least five centuries before the barbarian hordes swarmed into the western provinces the Romans had been aware of the danger of having on their frontiers these truculent and restless tribesmen, who were attracted by the wealth of the Empire, its fertile fields and rich cities. In the last years of the second century B.C. they invaded Gaul and northern Italy, but the victories of Marius forced them to turn back. A half-century later Caesar's legions halted the Germanic tribes threatening Gaul, but the menace remained, and Augustus, the first Roman emperor, tried to create a safer frontier by conquering and annexing all the territory between the Rhine and Elbe Rivers. When the barbarians inflicted a humiliating defeat on his army, the Romans retired to the Rhine and established their northern defenses from that river to the Black Sea along the course of the Danube. Thereafter, save for limited annexations of territory, notably the addition of Dacia, the Romans were content to maintain this boundary. Until the reign of Marcus Aurelius the Roman system of defenses was strong enough to keep the barbarians from breaking into the Empire, and except for border incidents and skirmishes, barbarians and Romans coexisted peacefully.

From Marcus' time the Germans tried again and again to push their way across the frontier. The Marcomannic Wars were only the first in a series of costly wars waged by Rome in order to prevent the forcible entry of the barbarian hordes. Henceforth the Empire was on the defensive, and one of its major problems in the disastrous third century was to maintain its integrity against these wandering tribes. We have seen how during that century the northern defenses had collapsed and the barbarians had surged into the frontier provinces and beyond. Only the brilliant victories of the soldier-emperors, Claudius Gothicus and Aurelian, had saved the Empire from destruction. The Gothic danger was averted, but only temporarily, and on the frontiers, contracted after the abandonment of

Dacia, the presence of the Germans always reminded the Romans how precarious were the dikes which they had raised against them. The floods came in the following century, and all the efforts of the Romans were powerless to keep them from inundating the Western Empire and threatening the Eastern Empire.

The barbarians had no blueprint for conquest, and, so far as we know, no desire to overthrow the Roman Empire. For centuries they had been migrating in search of new lands, since with their rudimentary system of agriculture they were unable to reduce enough of the forest and swamp areas which they inhabited to provide them with sufficient food for an expanding population. Until the last quarter of the fourth century the Romans were generally able to contain them, since the movements of the Germans were isolated and unco-ordinated and the Roman defenses strong enough to keep them out. Now the pressures became sharper as the Germans themselves felt the thrust of a still more barbaric people. Pushing in panic upon the Roman frontiers, they discovered the weakness of the Empire and advanced until they gained most of western Europe.

The Role of the Huns

The great invasions were set in motion around 375 by the appearance of the Huns, who had swept westward two decades or so earlier from the steppes of central Asia into eastern Europe. These mounted nomads, repulsive in appearance, savage and restless in manner, terrified Germans and Romans alike. Because of an extraordinary mobility which enabled them to make whirlwind raids here and then there, their numbers were greatly exaggerated. Nevertheless, they were a formidable host, and their attacks drove the panic-stricken Germans across the Roman frontiers of the Rhine and the Danube. The first to feel the impact of the Huns were the Ostrogoths, who were pushed back of the Dniester River around 370 and overwhelmed in 375. Then the Visigoths, unable to defend themselves, obtained permission to settle on Roman territory south of the Danube. But outraged by the highhanded treatment given them by the Roman officials who were charged with their reception, they rose in rebellion, pillaged the countryside, and in the battle of Adrianople in 378 annihilated a great Roman army and then overran the whole Balkan Peninsula. Rome had suffered one of the most disastrous defeats in her history.

Racked by domestic difficulties, the Western Empire was unable to offer effective resistance to the advancing barbarians. The Eastern Empire, shielded by the sea and the strategic location of Constantinople and protected by stronger armies and even more by a subtle diplomacy of bribes and threats, escaped the brunt of attack, which was diverted westward. The Rhine and Danube defenses now crumbled under the irresistible pressure of the barbarians, and the German hordes, Vandals, Alemanni, Ostrogoths, Burgundians, and Franks, flooded into the Empire. The weak Western Roman emperors withdrew to their new capital at Ravenna and left German commanders like Stilicho and Ricimer to defend Italy. A century after Adrianople the Visigoths controlled Spain and part of Gaul; the Ostrogoths Italy; the Franks and Burgundians shared the rest of Gaul; the Vandals ruled Africa, and the Angles and Saxons were conquering Britain. The West had fallen.

While the Visigoths, Vandals, and other Germanic groups were creating their kingdoms in the Roman West, the savage Huns, who had driven the Visigoths to seek safety behind the Roman frontiers in 375, broke down all opposition. When in 450 the Romans refused to pay them further tribute, the Huns started a relentless conquest of Europe which carried them from the lower Danube to Gaul. Visigoths and Romans joined forces to stem their advance, and in 451 at the battle of Campus Mauriacus, near Troyes in Gaul, the Huns were defeated and turned back. Two years later, with the death of Attila, their dread leader, their empire collapsed and they ceased to threaten Europe. The advance of the Germanic nations, however, continued unchecked.

German Rule in the West

The Germans had not set out to destroy the Empire; what they wanted from Rome was land and protection from their own enemies. Pressure of the Huns had forced the Goths to begin that peaceful migration into the Empire which turned into attack and forcible entry and conquest. Once the weakness of Rome was exposed, the invasions began. Actually the number of invaders was relatively small. The smaller groups ranged from 25,000 to 50,000; the larger groups from 80,000 to 120,000, of whom only 20 per cent were fighting men. In some of the pitched battles between Romans and Germans, therefore, as few as 10,000 to 20,000 men were engaged on either side. The invaders as a whole represented perhaps no more than 5 per cent of the Roman provincial population whose lands they appropriated and among whom they settled. But the Roman armies were largely barbarian in composition and fought only halfheartedly, and Rome's citizens had neither the will nor the capacity to resist. Rome succumbed not so much to the barbarian invasions as to that internal malady which has been described in the preceding chapter.

By the beginning of the sixth century the barbarians were firmly established in the lands of the Western Roman Empire. In a little more than a century they had crossed the Rhine and the Danube and created their own states in the western provinces. What had been the nature of the invasions? What was the fate of the Roman and provincial population? Aside from the immediate destruction of Roman control in the West, what were the results of the clash of the two peoples?

Invasion by Infiltration

The Roman Empire was not overwhelmed by a sudden catastrophic invasion of German hordes. There were, to be sure, several occasions in the past when large German forces had defeated Roman armies and moved into Roman territory. But in general the barbarian occupation was a slow process of infiltration which had been going on ceaselessly for several centuries. The Roman government itself had settled large groups of barbarians in the frontier areas, enrolled thousands of them in the army, and accepted whole tribes as allies who promised in return for grants of land to guard the frontier against other Germans.

There were peaceful contacts as well as warlike relations between the two neighboring peoples. In the frontier districts Romans and Germans lived side by side, and each came naturally to have some knowledge of the other. Roman merchants crossed the border into German lands in search of new markets and fresh sources of supply and introduced the barbarians to Roman products and ways. Neither the German immigrants nor their kinsmen across the frontier were more than superficially Romanized, but their manner of life was altered as a result of these contacts. The rough edges of German culture were rubbed smooth by Roman influence, and Roman culture itself changed subtly as increasing numbers of Germans were absorbed into the Empire. Thus the two cultures had begun to blend to a considerable extent even before the period of mass migrations.

Economic Activity

With thousands of people on the march, with fighting and bloodshed, there was inevitably enormous material damage and destruction and a disruption of the normal way of life. Men were slain, cities ravaged and looted, villas destroyed, fields untilled, flocks and herds carried off. Economic activity was paralyzed and conditions as a whole were chaotic until the invaders settled down and established their states.

Trade and commerce, already declining in the Later Roman Empire, as we have seen, suffered a still more serious setback, and urban life decayed. Some Roman cities were abandoned by their terror-stricken inhabitants; others survived merely as convenient centers for the transaction of civil and ecclesiastical administrative affairs. In agriculture, however, there was a recovery as the once pastoral and nomadic barbarians settled down and turned to farming. The system of large estates owned by nobles and worked by *coloni* was adopted by the invaders, who largely replaced the Romans as landowners. Thereby an important element of the institutional heritage of Rome was transmitted by the Germanic conquerors to the mediaeval world.

Coalescence of German and Roman Culture

Although Roman and barbarian now lived side by side, each influencing the other, there were serious obstacles to cultural coalescence. The two peoples had different origins, languages, religious beliefs, political and social institutions; they stood on different levels of cultural development. But in general the Germans admired and respected Rome, displayed a tolerance and forebearance toward Roman ways, and made a determined effort to preserve Roman civilization. Instead of imposing their own culture upon the conquered Romans, they allowed them to retain many of their own laws and institutions. Hence the two peoples lived together more or less amicably, each with their own laws, language, and religion, until a process of cultural fusion brought them more closely together and blurred the distinctions. In short, Roman civilization was greatly weakened, but it was not destroyed.

One source of hostility between Romans and Germans was the difference in religious beliefs. At the time of the invasions most of the Germans had become Christians, having been converted soon after 340 by Wulfila, or Ulfilas, a Goth who had lived in Constantinople as a hostage and had there been ordained as a bishop. Wulfila, the so-called "Apostle of the Goths," translated the Bible into Gothic for his people, and despite opposition, Christianity spread widely among them. Wulfila, however, had belonged to the Arian sect whose beliefs were condemned at the Council of Nicaea. Having originally accepted this heretical form of Christianity, the Germans retained it long after it had been rejected by the majority of Romans. Thus religion widened the gulf between the two peoples. In Gaul, however, the Franks, under their king Clovis, accepted orthodox Christianity at the end of the fifth century and the union of Germanic conquerors and Gallo-Roman subjects was facilitated.

In the course of time the invaders took over more and more of the institutions and customs of the conquered Romans: administrative practices and devices, the municipal system, taxes, Roman law and law courts, the Latin language for governmental purposes and literary expression, the orthodox Christian religion. Most important of all, they accepted the imperial ideal, the belief in the power and the glory of Rome and the Roman Empire. It is significant that such powerful German rulers as Theodoric, king of the Ostrogoths in Italy, and Clovis, king of the Franks in Gaul, took legitimate title to their lands from the Roman emperors at Constantinople, the only emperors now that the Western Empire had ceased to exist. In other ways, too, the new masters of western Europe demonstrated their acceptance of the imperial tradition. For them the Roman Empire, the western half of which they themselves had helped to destroy, had never really perished; Rome was still the Eternal City. Given a new meaning in the church and in the Holy Roman Empire of the Middle Ages, the belief in the survival of Rome remained a potent force, perhaps the most important part of the Roman legacy to the mediaeval world.

The Fusion of Roman and Germanic Elements

Although never complete, there was a fusion of the two cultures, the later Roman and the German. In effecting the synthesis, the Christian church played a major role, adapting itself to the new situation, sometimes exercising in those troubled times the only effective political authority, tempering the roughness of the barbarians, and helping to civilize them by introducing them to Roman culture. Learning, literature, and art suffered during the chaotic years of the great invasions, but they did not die. While it was principally the church which kept ancient culture alive, the German kings themselves, and especially Theodoric of Ostrogothic Italy, preserved the framework and much of the content of Roman civilization. Whatever their faults and weaknesses from the point of view of the golden age of Latin literature, such writers as the philosopher Boethius and the scholar-administrator Cassiodorus in Ostrogothic Italy, the encyclopedist Isidore of Seville in Visigothic Spain, the poets Sidonius Apollinaris and Fortunatus in Gaul, and the historian of the Franks, Gregory of Tours, show the abiding strength of the classical tradition. In the magnificent mosaics of Italy and in the jewelry of Gaul and Spain, Roman influences also predominated. Europe suffered heavy losses, and a large part of the civilized world reverted to barbarism during this age of transition. But much of the Roman cultural heritage was salvaged and accepted by the German conquerors of western Europe and preserved by them for later generations.

The Eastern Roman Empire

The Western Roman Empire perished and in its place the German kingdoms were established. The Eastern Roman Empire, however, survived, and for a thousand years, from the fifth to the fifteenth centuries, flourished as a great world power, stable when western Europe was anarchic, civilized when the West was groping its way out of the darkness of the early Middle Ages. In their capital at Constantinople, as heirs of Augustus, the eastern emperors strove to uphold the Roman imperial ideal. To them the western world, the Slavic world, and the Moslem world owe a large debt for their zealous preservation of the heritage of classical antiquity. But the Eastern Roman Empire was more than a guardian of the classical tradition. Out of their own genius, from Greek, Roman, Oriental, and Christian elements, its people created the rich and brilliant civilization which is called Byzantine after Byzantium, the older name of Constantinople.

Constantine the Great had chosen a magnificent site for his new capital. Here in Constantinople, as Gibbon says, "The prospect of beauty, of safety, and of wealth were united in a single spot." Controlling the land route from Europe to Asia and the sea route from the Black Sea to the Mediterranean, protected by the sea on two sides and fortifications on the third side, the city was easy to defend and remained unconquered for over a thousand years. Equally well situated for trade, Constantinople became the most prosperous city of the mediaeval world. Until its capture by the Turks in 1453 this great cosmopolitan city was a beacon light of Graeco-Roman culture.

The Division of the Empire

Constantine ruled over a united Roman Empire and his successors sought to maintain that unity. But when Theodosius divided the Empire between his two sons in 395, the separation into a western and an eastern empire, foreshadowed by Diocletian's administrative division a century earlier, was definitely established. The distinction between a Latin West and a Greek East was increasingly marked, as Greek tended to supplant Latin as the official language in the East, and as differences developed within the church in the two regions. In theory, however, the Empire remained one and indivisible, and to the abiding strength of that belief in a single empire may be attributed the grandiose project of the emperor Justinian (527–565) to reconstitute the Empire by winning back from the barbarians the lost western provinces.

Although the Eastern Empire escaped the brunt of the barbarian attacks and suffered less than the West, its territories were also ravaged by successive hordes of invaders: Visigoths, Huns, Ostrogoths, and Slavs and Bulgars later. It had, moreover, the task of defending its eastern frontiers against Persia. Like the West, the East had internal weaknesses inherited in part from the Later Roman Empire: palace intrigues and revolts, weak emperors, insubordinate generals who were often of barbarian origin, corrupt civil servants, and mercenary armies levied among the barbarians. Despite these weaknesses, the Eastern Empire successfully resisted the barbarians, bribed them to move elsewhere or drove them off. However great the threat, Constantinople remained an impregnable bastion of the state. But there were other elements of strength too: a conciliatory foreign policy toward Persia, which for a time relieved the pressure on the eastern frontier and enabled the emperors to concentrate on western problems; an important reservoir of fighting men in Asia Minor; a generally efficient bureaucracy; prosperous cities and a flourishing industry and commerce which helped to finance the government. So the East was able to weather the worst storms of the fourth and fifth centuries, and in the sixth century to take the offensive under the emperor Justinian.

Justinian

Fifty years before Justinian mounted the throne in Constantinople the last Western emperor had been deposed and German kings ruled in his place. Although Justinian was a Roman emperor, his control extended only to the Adriatic. The western provinces seemed irretrievably lost. Yet so intense was his belief in the divinely inspired mission of a Roman emperor that he set himself resolutely to reconquer these provinces and to restore imperial unity under his rule. The attempt was only partially successful and the cost very high. But never again was a Roman emperor to rule over as wide an empire, an empire which once more stretched along the western shores of the Mediterranean. Whatever his failure, then, Justinian may be regarded as one of the greatest figures of Europe in the age of transition.

The splendid mosaics in the Church of San Vitale in Ravenna give us a vivid portrait of Justinian and his empress, Theodora. The personalities, the characters, and the achievements of the imperial couple are presented even more graphically by Procopius, a contemporary historian. Justinian was a vain and stubborn ruler, ambitious for power and glory, and tireless in his autocratic concern for administrative, military, and theological problems. In his various enterprises he was supported by his brilliant and beautiful wife Theodora, who rose from humble origins and a scandalous past to become until her death in 548 his ablest assistant and virtually coruler.

The recovery of the lost provinces of the West was a goal of the imperial policy which Justinian pursued with grim determination. Not long after his accession he commissioned

Belisarius, his best general, to reconquer Africa from the Vandals. In 533, after a year's fighting, Africa was again a Roman province, but revolts and mutinies prolonged the war until 548, when Roman authority was made secure. Meantime, in 535, Belisarius began the recovery of Italy from the Ostrogoths, and by 540 Gothic resistance was broken. But when Belisarius was withdrawn, the Goths under their king Totila rose in revolt and drove the Roman garrisons from nearly the whole peninsula. Not until 554 was Roman authority re-established in Italy by the brilliant Eastern Roman general, Narses. The country was all but devastated after the long years of war and Rome itself a shambles from siege, capture, and recapture. Southern Spain and the Mediterranean islands were also reconquered by Justinian's generals, but no more was attempted, if indeed the emperor had ever proposed to retake all the lost territory. Gaul remained firmly under Frankish control, most of Spain under the Visigoths, and Britain under warring barbarians.

Justinian's plans for westward expansion could only be accomplished if the eastern and northern frontiers were stabilized. Since he had only limited resources of men and money, the corollary of an aggressive policy in the West had to be a defensive one elsewhere. This the emperor tried to establish by erecting a strong system of walls and fortifications, by bribing and subsidizing barbarians and Persians, and by a devious diplomacy which was designed to keep his enemies at war with one another. The policy was costly and unsuccessful and wars had to be fought in the East as in the West. Huns, Slavs, and other barbarians broke through the Danube defenses and overran the Balkan Peninsula, although they were kept away from Constantinople.

Meanwhile, the provinces on the eastern frontier suffered heavily from Persian raids and full-scale fighting. Justinian's program of reconstituting the old Roman Empire resulted in no lasting gain in the West, jeopardized the heart of the Empire which was in the East, and imposed an almost intolerable burden upon his hard-pressed subjects.

The Problem of Heresy

The re-establishment of political unity was only one part of the emperor's program. "Governing under the authority of God," as he expressed it in his laws, Justinian regarded it as equally his duty to achieve religious uniformity in his domains. Indeed, religion and politics were two facets of the same imperial policy, and the Vandal and Ostrogothic wars were waged not merely to regain lost provinces, but also to free the orthodox church from domination by heretical Germans. Both in the West and in the East force and persuasion were employed against the surviving pagans and various groups of heretical Christians. Against paganism, which drew its devotees chiefly from the educated classes, Justinian struck a mortal blow by closing the Academy and the Lyceum, the philosophical schools of Athens which had maintained an unbroken tradition of pagan learning from the days of their founders, Plato and Aristotle. Against heretics in Africa and Italy he proceeded aggressively, once these lands had been reconquered.

The most serious problem, however, was presented by the Monophysite Christians in the provinces of Egypt and Syria. Ostensibly their heresy was concerned with the definition of the nature of Christ (see page 127). But the Monophysite heresy was also a rallying point for those who were discontented with the imperial regime. The controversy became one aspect of a growing political, economic, and cultural conflict between the native population of Egypt and Syria and the Graeco-Roman ruling class, whom they regarded as alien oppressors. For Justinian, the Monophysite problem was baffling: the attempt to satisfy their demands, as urged by Theodora, placated the eastern provinces but antagonized the orthodox elements in the Empire, especially the papacy, and jeopardized the success of the imperial foreign policy in the West. The emperor wavered between persecution and appeasement of the Monophysites and sought formulas of compromise. In the end he failed to satisfy the eastern provinces, which were increasingly disaffected, or the western provinces, which were alienated by his concessions to heretics.

More successful was his encouragement of missionary activity, which carried both Christianity and the culture of the Eastern Roman Empire from Constantinople to regions far outside the Empire and eventually endowed the Slavic peoples of Russia and the Balkans with a rich legacy of Byzantine art, literature, and learning. Byzantine culture is, in fact, an essential basis of the civilization of the Slavic world.

Justinian's absolutism in the sphere of ecclesiastical affairs, his attempts to legislate for the church, his interest and active participation in doctrinal disputes, in short, his effort to treat the church as a department of the state, is sometimes called "Caesaropapism." That term, which implies that the emperor was head of the church as well as of the state, may be inaccurate, but it serves nevertheless to underscore his conviction that his powers transcended those of any other person or institution. Although to a large extent Justinian controlled the church in the East and made it an organ of the state, the stubborn resistance of orthodox Christians to his efforts to reach an accommodation with the Monophysites indicates that the church was by no means completely subservient to his will.

The Cost of Imperial Government

Justinian's rule was absolute, but he needed help to govern a great and even growing empire. His administrative machinery was a version of the complex bureaucracy which he inherited from the Later Roman Empire, expanded by a host of high ministers and lesser officials in a hierarchy of rank and position. An army of civil servants assisted these officials. But as in the Later Empire, corruption was rife, offices were bought and sold, only a fraction of the taxes reached the treasury, and all the efforts of the emperor to introduce administrative reforms failed.

The root of the evil was his constant need for money. His costly wars and diplomacy, his extravagant building program and elaborate court life, could only be paid for by increasingly higher levies. Regardless of his subjects' inability to pay or the venality of the officials, money had to be raised. All this strained the economic structure of the realm. The treasury was exhausted, the currency debased, and still taxes were multiplied. As in the Later Roman Empire, the burden lay heaviest on the humbler classes of peasants and city-folk; the great landowners were able to escape the demands of the state.

From the very outset of Justinian's reign there was widespread antagonism to his fiscal policies. The famous Nika Riots of 532, so-called from the slogan *Nika* or "Conquer!" shouted by the mobs, were a sudden explosion of pentup dissatisfaction with the government. The riots began as a

quarrel between the factions which supported rival chariot-
eers in the races held in the hippodrome. But since these
circus factions represented at the same time conflicting religious and political views, the Nika Riots soon became an
open rebellion which threatened the safety of the emperor
himself. Only by the iron courage of Theodora was Justinian kept from abdicating and were the riots finally
quelled. He undertook fresh reforms, but none was effective as long as his need for money remained pressing. By
the end of his reign the army was dangerously reduced, the
fortresses were neglected, and the Persians and barbarians
were kept out of the Empire only by heavy bribes for
which more money had to be found. The western conquests, incomplete in any event, exhausted the state. When
after Justinian's death in 565 the Lombards advanced into
Italy, the Eastern Empire was too weak to prevent these
new German invaders from establishing a kingdom there.
Within a century, too, most of the other western conquests
were abandoned to the armies of Islam, while in the East,
Egypt and Syria offered no firm resistance to conquest first
by the Persians and eventually by the Arabs.

Justinian's vaulting ambitions brought the Eastern Roman Empire close to ruin. His conquests were ephemeral,
his religious policy a failure. But Justinian is remembered
less for these failures than for two magnificent achievements: a code of laws, which preserved for later generations in the West as well as the East the finest product of the
Roman genius, and the Church of St. Sophia, the greatest
monument of Byzantine art.

Corpus Iuris Civilis

For more than a thousand years the Romans, through
their assemblies, magistrates, emperors, and lawyers, had

been fashioning a system of law which was designed to ensure justice for the individual and stability for the state. In its conservatism Roman law reflected the Roman character itself, but as the Roman character was molded by changing circumstances, so the law was modified to meet new situations created by the historical development of Rome: the acquisition of an empire and successive changes in her government, economy, and society. Civil law, which applied to Roman citizens, had broadened out in time to include the concept of a law of nations, as the Romans recognized an obligation to provide justice for noncitizens as well as citizens in their world-empire and as they realized that other legal systems, the laws and customs of other peoples, might be tapped to furnish a basis for a wider law than their own. From the time of the Late Republic a succession of brilliant lawyers had studied the law, given interpretations of it, and sought the principles underlying it. They had tempered its firmness with fairness, and rendered it more flexible, more equitable, and more humane. Through the influence of Stoic philosophy the Romans came to have a vision of a still broader and more fundamental law, a law of nature lying back of civil law and the law of nations. Here, however imperfectly glimpsed, was the law existing in nature not for Romans alone or for Greeks or Germans, but for all men everywhere and always. The lawyers, many of whom were Stoics, looked behind Roman law and sought to approach that law of nature of which manmade law was only an approximation. Paradoxically it was in the autocratic Later Empire that Roman law became more humane, more equitable, and more universal under the impact of these intellectual interests and of Christianity itself.

Long before Justinian's time the great period of creative activity in Roman law had ended, but much remained to be

done if it were to be a living and usable force. Not only was
there a great mass of legal enactments going back to early
Republican times and continued by the emperors, but there
were also the interpretations of the law, made by such
jurists as Ulpian, Papinian, and Paulus, which had become
an intrinsic part of Roman law. The general structure of the
law was sound and impressive, but in detail it was ambigu-
ous, repetitious, and obsolete—a natural result of its long
development. The lawyers had often rendered contradic-
tory interpretations, and successive emperors had issued
conflicting enactments. An attempt had been made by Emperor Theodosius II to create some order out of this chaos,
and his Theodosian Code (438) at least codified and clari-
fied the edicts of the emperors beginning with Constantine,
and in time it provided the barbarian kingdoms with a basic
code for Romans in their dominions. Much still remained
to be done, however, if a path were to be cut through the
tangled thicket of law. Soon after his accession to the throne
Justinian undertook the task as one phase of his program
of administrative reform. To accomplish it he appointed
a commission of distinguished lawyers, who produced the
Codex Justinianus, a revised and systematic code of all imperial laws which were still in force. Justinian's *Digest* or
Pandects, published soon afterward, provided a harmonious
and usable compilation of the vast literature of legal interpretations made by the jurists. The *Institutes* was designed
to serve as an elementary textbook for students of law,
and the *Novellae* included laws issued by Justinian after the
publication of the *Codex*.

In his great work of systematizing and crystallizing the
law, Justinian wrought not merely for his time but for the
ages. The *Corpus Iuris Civilis*, as his codification came to

be called, preserves in living form Rome's greatest heritage. It is a permanent record of Rome's equity and justice and a guide to thought and action for later generations.

The Church of St. Sophia

The magnificent Church of St. Sophia remains today, nearly 1,500 years after it was erected in Constantinople by order of Justinian, one of the world's priceless treasures. The vast dome floating in mid-air, as it were, the pillars and walls of colored marble and the glowing mosaics which pick up and reflect the flood of light from the windows, all create an unforgettable impression of harmony, splendor, and beauty. Like the *Corpus Iuris Civilis*, St. Sophia endured long after Justinian and the Eastern Roman Empire. These two achievements epitomize the mission of that empire: to preserve the legacy of the ancient world—whether in art or law—and to blend the classical with the Christian.

Problems Confronting the Christian Church

Underlying all else in this age of transition in the East and the West, in the Roman Empire and the Germanic kingdoms alike, was the hard bedrock of the Christian church. By the end of the fourth century the church was triumphant, but it had to face and solve a number of problems. Some were posed within its ranks by the very fact of its success; others were presented from outside by the events of the period. So the church had to develop an administrative organization adequate for a rapidly growing institution and in some measure capable of dealing with problems which were once the concern of the state, but which were now, in the vacuum created by the decline of the Western Roman Empire, the concern of the church.

The increasing need for a centralized organization which could provide solidarity and cohesion led to the creation of a hierarchical government for the church and to the rise of the sovereign papacy. The conquest of the West by barbarians who had already accepted the Christian religion or were soon to do so meant that Christianity was no longer coterminous with the Roman world, but had become a supernational religion. The church had, therefore, to determine its relations with a host of separate states, Roman and German. As the ties which bound East and West weakened, the church found it more difficult to maintain unity in its own ranks. In the face of spreading heresy a firm statement of Christian doctrine had to be made. Here the church Fathers, the great theologians and spokesmen of the early centuries, played a major role in combating heresy and in stating clearly the orthodox belief, while church councils provided authoritative rulings on disputed questions. Finally, as the church grew in numbers, strength, and wealth, what seemed to be its increasing worldliness disturbed many of the faithful, and some tried to escape the world and its ways by adopting ascetic practices. The development of the monastic movement presented the church with the problem of controlling and directing these impulses and tendencies.

Paganism

In spite of the victory of Christianity in the fourth century, staunch supporters of the pagan gods were still to be found among the country folk, who were traditionally conservative, and among intellectuals and aristocrats, who had been reared on a literature which was rooted in paganism. It was during the reign of an emperor who was both an aristocrat and an intellectual that paganism enjoyed a brief revival. Soon after he became emperor, Julian (361–363), the so-called Apostate, rebelled against the Christian faith and tried to replace it by a pagan religion which incorporated some of the institutions and practices of Christianity. At the same time he took discriminatory measures against the Christians by means of which he hoped to destroy their religion. His pagan cult, with its blend of pagan and Christian practices and Greek philosophy, had, however, little real vitality, and the reasons which had won men to Christianity were as cogent as before. This final attempt to infuse new life into the old religion failed, and Julian's paganism died with him. The temples of the gods were soon closed or were converted to other uses or fell into ruin. By the end of the century legal toleration of paganism ceased and sacrifices to the pagan gods were prohibited as treasonable. The Roman Empire was now officially an orthodox Christian state, although paganism lingered in some circles until Justinian's time. But the death blow had been given long before, and all that remained of paganism were some practices which were adapted to Christianity and, more important, pagan literature and learning, in which the church Fathers were steeped and from which they borrowed not only many of the basic concepts of their thought, but the very modes of expression.

Development of Church Organization

In the early days of the Christian church a simple rudimentary organization sufficed for the separate communities of believers. Now that Christianity was victorious and claimed its converts everywhere in the Roman and barbarian world, a more elaborate ecclesiastical organization was

needed to give it strength and unity. Quite naturally the
church, which had come into being and won its victory
within the frontiers of the Empire, modeled its organization
upon the highly developed system already in existence in
the Roman world and adapted to its own needs Roman
methods, practices, and institutions. Distinctions between
clergy and laymen had developed very early, and these
tended to harden as the clergy assumed leadership over laity.
Within each city the bishops emerged as the church's chief
administrative officials. The Roman scheme of provincial
administration was also adopted, and when problems concerning Christians of a whole province arose, the bishops
met in the provincial capital under the leadership of the
metropolitan or archbishop of that city. Thus Christianity
became an institutional religion with an administrative
machinery which reproduced that of the Empire.

In the absence of a strong government the church stepped
into the breach and began to discharge civil functions. As
municipal government decayed, the bishop's prestige and
power grew and he often became the leading person in the
city. Not only did he have authority in the realm of religious affairs, but he came to possess recognized rights of
civil jurisdiction. In this role he served as an effective
counterweight to the arbitrary power of the imperial bureaucracy and protected men from oppression by the government. So, too, the church alleviated the distress of the
poor and provided hospitals and orphanages, in short, assumed many of the functions exercised in the days of
Rome's prosperity by the imperial or municipal government. The church had increasing resources for the performance of these charitable works, for in 321 Constantine
had decreed that it could accept gifts and legacies. Al-

though this wealth enabled the church to perform a variety of social services, it also posed fresh problems, which became acute as the patrimonies of the church swelled through the generosity of the faithful.

The Bishop of Rome

Early in the history of the church the bishops of Rome acquired great power and influence, and in time a succession of able bishops pressed their claim to sovereign power over the whole church. In part this was the logical outgrowth of the process of development by which the ecclesiastical organization was modeled on that of the Roman Empire. The capital of the Empire was appropriately enough regarded by many as the capital of the church, and just as the bishops of provincial capitals were considered as more important than other bishops, so the bishop of the imperial capital enjoyed special prestige. But a more important basis for the claim for the primacy of the Roman bishops or popes was the Petrine tradition, that is, that Christ had delegated sole and supreme authority to the apostle Peter, traditionally regarded as the founder of the church at Rome, and that the bishops of Rome, as apostolic successors of St. Peter, therefore possessed supreme authority over the church. The famous passage in Matthew 16:18–19 was quoted in support of the claim: "Thou art Peter [Petros], and upon this rock [*petra* in Greek] I will build my church." Although there was initial opposition from certain bishops elsewhere, the bishop of Rome won increasing acceptance as head of the church, and by 381 his primacy was officially recognized by the church council of Constantinople. Rome, no longer the capital of the Empire, was now the capital of the Christian church. In the vacuum created by the transfer and eventually by the fall of the imperial government in the West, the popes became more active in the administration and even in the defense of the city and achieved a sovereignty which extended from ecclesiastical to civil affairs.

The power of the papacy was greatly strengthened, and, indeed, the foundations of the mediaeval papacy were established by a series of able leaders: by Pope Leo I (440–461), who vigorously proclaimed the Petrine Doctrine; by Pope Gelasius I (492–496), who defended the theory of the supremacy of the church over the state; and finally by Pope Gregory the Great (590–604), who brought the whole orthodox Christian world in close connection with the See of Peter. While the Eastern Roman emperors were less willing than the German rulers of the West to recognize the supremacy of the popes, they co-operated with them and in many practical ways demonstrated their acceptance of papal supremacy. Thus by the sixth century the mediaeval conception of the dominant role of the papacy was solidly established.

Heresies

Even before it won its victory in the Roman world, alarming cracks had appeared in the structure of the church as controversies arose over the nature of Christian doctrine. Constantine had attempted to deal with the most dangerous of these disputes, the Arian controversy, which concerned the problem of the nature of Christ. Many Christians had accepted the teachings of Arius, a priest of Alexandria, that God and the Son were of like, but not identical, substance. Others, following Athanasius, the bishop of Alexandria, held that God and the Son were of the same substance and insisted that the Arian teachings relegated Christ to a secondary place. Although the theological questions were abstruse and complex, the controversy inflamed public opinion, especially in the East, and threatened to split both the church and the Empire into two irreconcilable parts. Constantine therefore tried to settle the question at the church council which met at Nicaea in 325. Here the teachings of Athanasius were proclaimed as orthodox and the Nicene Creed, which embodied them, was accepted, while the Arian views were condemned as heretical. Even though it was supported by the emperor, the publication of the Creed did not produce uniformity of belief, and many persisted in the Arian heresy or, like the German invaders of the Empire, were converted to Arian Christianity.

Disagreements about the nature of Christian doctrine continued despite the efforts of the church and sometimes the state to end controversy and to establish a universal Christian creed. The fifth-century heresies, which flourished chiefly in the Eastern Empire, were supported by those groups in the population which were already alienated from the government for political, social, economic, and cultural reasons. Hence, as the account of Justinian's reign has shown, it was difficult to heal the rifts that developed between Constantinople and the provinces of Syria and Egypt. Moreover, the problem was complicated because of the widening gap between the East and the West. A settlement which satisfied the eastern provinces alienated the church in the West, and a solution pleasing to Rome intensified the disruptive factors in the East. The Nestorian heresy, which stressed the human element in Christ, and the Monophysite heresy, which seemed to deny the human and to emphasize the divine element, were the chief heresies which plagued the Eastern Roman emperors. Nestorianism was proscribed by a church council and most of its adherents chose the path of exile, but Monophysitism proved less tractable, and the emperors, notably Justinian, could find no formula which would satisfy Constantinople, the eastern provinces, and the church at Rome. Persecution failed, as did compromise, and only the loss of Egypt and Syria settled the problem by removing the dissident elements. The price of religious uniformity was high, but by the end of the sixth century there was a net gain. A greater degree of cohesion had been won by separating the orthodox from the heretics, and in the course of the controversies the church had been compelled to define the articles of its faith clearly and forcefully.

The Monastic Movement

The church was called upon to solve another thorny problem in this age of transition: how to control or to guide the monastic movement which was spreading rapidly from its original home in the East to the West. Conditions within and outside the church were responsible for the popularity of monasticism. By flight to the monastic life men tried to escape or at least to bear more easily the evils of the Roman world, in which they were insecure, overburdened, and overtaxed. Among the monks were men who had been victimized by the absolutist Roman government, persecuted as Christians by a still pagan Empire, or in later times ruined by barbarian attack. Others sought in the solitude of the monk's life escape from what seemed to them to be the increasing worldliness of the church. In the desert or in lonely and inaccessible places they looked for peace and quiet where they might shun temptation, meditate and pray, and attain a life of holiness. For them the monastic life seemed the best path to salvation.

Monasticism had its origins in Egypt, where many chose to live as hermits in the desert or in the swamplands of the Nile Delta. But there were others who believed that only by mortification of the flesh through extreme ascetic practices could they demonstrate the ardor of their faith. The classic example is St. Simeon Stylites, who lived for some thirty years atop a pillar. A reaction to such extremes came, however, and the cenobitic or community form of monastic life superseded the anchoritic or solitary life of the hermit.

Monasticism soon spread from Egypt throughout the eastern Roman provinces. For these monastic foundations St. Basil (330–379) drew up a series of Rules which even today regulate monastic life in the Greek Church. His Rules stressed the importance of labor by the monks and, by minimizing the older emphasis upon harsh ascetic practices, gave monasticism a sane direction. Meanwhile the Roman emperors, who had first opposed the movement because it seemed to provide men with a means of escape from those civil and military obligations upon which the state depended, made their peace with monasticism.

The monastic ideal also spread from Egypt to the West and won acceptance, thanks largely to the work of St. Jerome. But the greatest figure of western monasticism was St. Benedict of Nursia (480–543), who drew up the Benedictine Rule for the government of the monastic community which he founded at Monte Cassino, near Rome. His practical code fixed for monks the three cardinal rules of poverty, chastity, and obedience, established an ordered life of labor and prayer, and provided methods for the administration of monasteries. For western monasticism the

Benedictine Rule came to be the accepted model, as St. Basil's Rules were for the East.

By their example the monks focused attention upon the other-worldly elements in Christianity. But Basil in the East and Benedict in the West made the monks aware of a part which they could play in the world, a role which would strengthen and not destroy their spiritual resolve. They became active missionaries who carried Christianity beyond the frontiers of the old Roman Empire. They maintained and improved old techniques of agriculture and helped to teach them to the barbarians. By founding libraries and by copying classical and Christian texts, they were largely responsible for preserving the literature and the learning of Greece and Rome.

The Conflict of Christian and Pagan Culture

Christianity had come into being and had spread in a pagan world. Its converts were drawn increasingly from those for whom Latin and Greek were native languages; in time its teachers and missionaries were men who knew the literature and philosophy of the classical world. Although a Christian education and literature developed, in the early centuries reliance was inevitably placed upon classical literature and learning. An obvious danger lurked here, that Christians might be corrupted or subverted by exposure to these pagan influences. What then was to be the attitude of the church? A clash of cultures, a struggle between two traditions, compromise, adjustment, and reconciliation: this in brief is the cultural history of the troubled age of transition. By the sixth century the conflict was fairly well resolved, not by the victory of a new

Christian culture over the older classical, but by a synthesis of the two cultures.

We have seen earlier that the decline of the Empire was reflected in the decline of pagan literature. The death of the pagan gods, who had loomed so large in ancient literature, removed one source of inspiration. But a more important deterrent to literary activity was the political, social, and economic crisis. Writers could seem to find little in their own society worth telling. Rhetorical adornment cloaked a poverty of ideas, and form rather than content became of supreme importance. On the whole pagan literature in the Later Roman Empire was pedantic and imitative, dull and colorless; it had reached a dead end. There were, however, exceptions in the fourth and fifth centuries. The poetry of Claudian and Rutilius Namatianus, heavily freighted though it is by rhetorical flourishes, is illuminated by flashes of talent and inspiration; while the history by Ammianus Marcellinus, who wrote in the latter half of the fourth century, is in the great tradition of Livy and Tacitus.

Long before this, confidence in science and reason had waned. Philosophy failed to attract or to hold men, and they turned instead to the mystery cults or to personal religions which appealed not to reason but to faith and emotion. Philosophy blended with religion and became scarcely distinguishable from it. In science, as in philosophy, no fresh creative work was accomplished. The uncritical compilations which were produced were crude and inadequate, but they represented much of the store of knowledge inherited by the early mediaeval world. So, too, the grammatical and rhetorical works of the period, notably the writings of Donatus, served the Middle Ages as stand-

ard textbooks and played an important part in the preservation of ancient learning.

In contrast to the pagan writers of the Later Empire the
Christian writers seemed to have fresh inspiration and
enthusiasm. Their religion provided them with a theme
which was vital and stimulating; new ideas, new interests,
and new spirit gave point and meaning to what they wrote.
In place of an essentially materialistic message Christianity
offered a spiritual one addressed to all men and not merely
to intellectuals or aristocrats. Christian authors, unlike their
pagan contemporaries, regarded it as their function to teach
and persuade rather than to please and entertain. Even before the victory of the church in the fourth century, therefore, Christian literature had begun to show more originality
and vigor than the pagan. In controversy with the defenders
of paganism and with heretics in their own ranks Christian
authors sharpened their weapons and acquired greater skill.
Eventually Christian literature superseded the pagan, but
not before it accepted its heritage.

A synthesis of the two cultures was effected only after
a long and bitter struggle. The sharp contrast between
pagan and Christian culture at first seemed to militate
against any reconciliation or compromise. Pagan intellectuals scorned Christian writers as crude and unlettered
flouters of pagan traditions. Christian authors in turn condemned much that they found in pagan literature: its allusions to gods and myths, its sensual appeal, its rationalism
and materialism, even its style, which seemed to seduce and
corrupt. The question which Tertullian asked in the second
century, "What have Athens and Jerusalem in common?"
epitomizes the Christian attitude. Christian writers suffered
pangs of conscience, but they continued to cherish classical

literature. St. Jerome portrays their mental conflict in his account of a dream in which Christ reproached him: "You are a Ciceronian, and not a Christian: where your treasure is, there is your heart also." [4]

Synthesis of the Two Cultures

A process of assimilation took place in the course of time; Christian writers accepted much of the classical tradition and employed it as one of the pillars upon which they erected the Christian culture of the Middle Ages. As Romans, they wrote and spoke in Latin or Greek. In the early centuries they were educated in Graeco-Roman schools, where pagan authors were the staple of instruction. They were thoroughly conversant with pagan literature and learning, and their thought and writings were naturally cast in a classical mold. They based their theological arguments on ancient philosophy and presented them in the familiar modes of ancient rhetoric. Eventually the Christians established their own schools, but the instruction offered in them stemmed from the classical. Inevitably Christian writers, whether brought up in classical or Christian schools, showed the influence of an education which was basically classical. They read Cicero, Virgil, Seneca, and other pagan authors, respected them and quoted them. Thus the two traditions, the classical and the Christian, were reconciled and harmonized in this age of transition, and out of the fusion mediaeval culture arose.

St. Jerome, St. Ambrose, and St. Augustine are the most distinguished but not the only Christian writers of the period which saw the decline of the Western Roman Empire and the rise of the German kingdoms. Jerome (347–

[4] Jerome, *Letters*, XXII, 30.

420), the most learned of the Latin Church Fathers, is best known for the Vulgate, his monumental translation of the Bible into Latin, but he produced translations of other works as well, scholarly commentaries on the Bible, and a whole library of theological treatises. In all his writings Jerome made it abundantly clear that he was both "Ciceronian" and "Christian." Although Ambrose (337–397) is best known for his practical administration as bishop of Milan, he was also a writer of distinction whose works show the strong influence of the classical authors upon a learned Christian. Even more marked was the impress of a classical education upon Augustine (354–430). His *Confessions*, which describes his own conversion, is one of the greatest of all spiritual autobiographies, and his *City of God*, which was inspired by the capture of Rome by the Visigoths in 410, is a magnificent account of universal history presented in terms of the contrast between the two cities, the transitory, earthly city of the world and the eternal, heavenly city of God.

The Christian poets, too, were stimulated by their classical training. Indeed, the poetry of Ausonius in the fourth century and of Sidonius Apollinaris in the following century is essentially pagan in inspiration or at least full of classical allusions. Even in the Christian hymns of Prudentius of Spain (348–405) the forms and techniques are still classical, although his ardent Christian faith gives these lyrical poems an intensity and sincerity which pagan poetry had lost.

Literary works of merit were still produced during the chaotic fifth and sixth centuries, when the Western Empire was overthrown and the Germanic kingdoms were founded. However debased the currency of classical learning and literature in the German realms, it continued to circulate. Boethius and Cassiodorus in Ostrogothic Italy, Gregory of Tours in Gaul, Isidore of Seville in Spain, and other writers kept alive the literary traditions which they inherited from the ancient world.

The conflict between pagan and Christian letters was resolved earlier in the East than in the West; indeed, it was never as intense. On the whole, the ancient tradition was cherished in the Greek East, and the sermons, theological tracts, poetry, and history produced there were indebted to pagan models for their style and thought. In so brief an essay we can only point to a few of the leading Greek writers—Basil the Great, Gregory of Nyssa, and Gregory of Nazianzus—who laid the foundations of Christian theology in the East during the fourth century; the ecclesiastical historian Eusebius (265–338), to whom the mediaeval world, West and East, was indebted for providing the techniques of historical writing as well as valuable historical data; and Procopius, the historian of Justinian's reign, the last of the great historians of the ancient world. As the Empire was sundered culturally as well as politically, the Greek language and literature all but vanished in the West, but in the Eastern Roman Empire the strength of the Hellenic tradition was demonstrated for a thousand years by a succession of Greek writers.

Assimilation in Art and Architecture

In general, those characteristics which we have observed in the literature of a dying paganism and of a triumphant Christianity can also be seen in art. The decline of the Empire was accompanied by a decline of old standards in art. Architects, sculptors, and painters were less and less influenced by classical canons of taste and technique. Where earlier artists had been concerned with moderation and balance, the artists of the Later Empire tried to achieve their effects by colossal size, whether of buildings or statues, bright and even garish colors, and a profusion of ornament and decoration. Nevertheless, the art of the period cannot be condemned as wholly decadent; on the contrary, in those very centuries something like an artistic renaissance occurred. As in literature, so in art, Christianity provided a new creative impulse, a new purpose, and new themes. As the church emerged triumphant, it needed places of worship worthy of a victorious religion; it called for statues, paintings, and mosaics to represent the Christian symbols and the central figures of Christianity, to teach the faith, and to narrate the Bible stories and the history of the church. No more than the Christian writer could escape the influence of pagan literature could the Christian artist avoid making use of the familiar forms, methods, and techniques of the pagan world of art. The older artistic forms were adapted to Christian uses and given a new vitality and a new spiritual meaning by the religious fervor of Christianity. Thus the Christian artists preserved the classical tradition and transformed it into the artistic traditions of the Byzantine East and the mediaeval West.

For the style of the churches the architects turned not to Roman temples, which were too small, and tainted besides with pagan associations, but to the basilica, a long rectangular building which the Romans had used successfully for law courts and other public business. They converted this basic form to Christian uses, varied it by adding main and subsidiary apses, aisles, and transepts, adorned it with ornate columns and capitals, arches, and decoration.

For the plan of their baptistries and churches the architects borrowed from Roman and perhaps Oriental domed structures, but they used these models in an original and creative manner. Whatever the style of architecture, the builders tried to demonstrate their devotion to their faith by painting, sculpture, and, above all, by magnificent mosaic pictures and decoration. In all these artistic forms they learned from Roman models and prototypes. In the minor arts too, in ivory carving, glassware, metalware, engraved stone, and jewelry, we see the same blending of the classical and the Christian, although other influences came in from the Orient and the barbarian world.

Synthesis of Roman, Germanic, and Christian Elements

We have traced through the age of transition the development of the three major elements out of which the civilization of the Middle Ages was fashioned. By the end of the period a rough and tentative synthesis of the old and the new, the Roman, Germanic, and Christian, had been achieved in the art and literature, in the politics, economy, and society of the western world. The synthesis is mediaeval civilization.

The world at the end of the sixth century was immensely altered. The Roman Empire had long before split into the Eastern and the Western Empires. The Western Empire in turn had disintegrated into the German kingdoms. But the Christian church gave men a common loyalty and a devotion to a single institution transcending empires and kingdoms. Through the Eastern Roman Empire, the German states of western Europe, and above all the church, mediaeval Europe received the institutional and intellectual heritage of the ancient world.

CHAPTER VI

The Roman Legacy

THE story of the rise and decline of Rome has stirred the imagination of mankind. In the thousand years of her history Rome, originally a small farming community, had emerged first as master of Italy and finally as ruler of the western world. Her people had consolidated the Empire under the Roman peace and buttressed it for centuries by an efficient system of administration and defense. Latin culture had been modified as a result of exposure to intellectual and artistic crosscurrents from the Graeco-Oriental parts of the Empire, and out of an amalgam of Oriental, Greek, and Roman elements the Romans had created a civilization of high order. The Roman achievement was magnificent; the Roman failure to meet the challenge presented by new experiences and to solve the problems posed by fresh responsibilities was disastrous.

By A.D. 600 peace and unity were shattered and the Roman Empire had disintegrated. In the four centuries from Marcus Aurelius to Justinian the Empire experienced civil war and anarchy, barbarian invasions, and political and economic crises. The Western Empire ceased to exist, and upon its territories the Germanic peoples created their kingdoms. Eastern Roman emperors still ruled from their capital at Constantinople, but over a greatly shrunken empire. The physical decline of Rome was accompanied by a deterioration of her civilization as the ancient structure of thought weakened. The Roman gods, who had been closely identified with Roman civilization and with the state itself, were vanquished by Christianity, whose victory heralded a new epoch.

The Survival of the Empire

Confronted by all the profound material and spiritual changes which constitute the phenomenon described as the decline of the Roman Empire, one may well ask not why that empire declined, but rather how it was able to endure for so long. There were weaknesses in the Empire, as we have seen, but there were obviously also enormous reserves of strength. The unity which Rome imposed upon the Mediterranean world and the administrative system and the law which held the Empire together enabled her to resist for a long time the forces of disintegration. These institutions which served Rome so well endured as an important part of the Roman legacy. Roman civilization as a whole was greatly altered, but it survived the crises of the Later Empire and lived on as an integral element of mediaeval and modern civilization. Rome's triumphs and successes were canceled by her failure, but what she accomplished in diverse areas of endeavor was not lost. In the long perspective of history the survival of Roman civilization, the heritage which generation after generation has accepted, is perhaps more significant than the decline of Rome.

Rome's genius was essentially practical, and it was preeminently in the domain of administration that the Roman legacy was greatest. The Greeks had failed to achieve political unity and had exhausted their strength in inter-state warfare; the Romans, on the contrary, succeeded in building a world-state. By force, diplomacy, and sometimes by chicanery—one may not gloss over the story—the Romans unified the ancient world. For a congeries of antagonistic and mutually warring states Rome substituted the *Pax Romana*, safeguarded by an army, but secured even more by law and by a variety of administrative devices fairly and efficiently applied. The solidly founded political system which Rome extended over her vast empire was the institutional heritage which she bequeathed to later ages.

The Chief Legacies

To the Eastern Roman Empire, which continued Rome's rule over a reduced area, to the barbarian states which took the place of the Western Roman Empire, and to the Christian church, Rome handed on the practices of government. The Eastern Roman emperors who ruled in almost unbroken sequence until the fall of Constantinople in 1453 accepted and maintained Roman principles of statecraft, and the German kings of western Europe likewise found in the Later Roman Empire a model for their absolute rule. They retained many of the features of the Roman administrative system: Roman imperial offices and perhaps municipal institutions, Roman titles and symbols of authority, the Roman system of public finances, Roman coin types, and above all, Roman law. From Rome too during these centuries the church received its basic organization, administration, and law. In the East and the West, church and state accepted the rich institutional heritage of Rome and thus perpetuated the ideals and traditions of the Roman state.

More important than any of these administrative practices was the Roman legacy in the realm of political ideals: common citizenship, political unity, a well-organized state living under law. Whatever the forms of government in their long history, whether monarchy or republic, the Principate of the Early Empire or the absolute, bureaucratic rule of the Later Empire, the Romans showed a virtual passion for these ideals. Long after the decline of the Empire they endured as Rome's major bequest to the world.

Roman citizenship had been extended to more and more of the inhabitants of the Empire until by the time of the emperor Caracalla (A.D. 212) it was almost universally held by free men. There were divisive forces which sundered East and West and separated the provinces from each other and from Italy itself. Nevertheless, in the great age of the Roman Empire a unified state was created out of peoples of different origins, and within the broad area of imperial unity local diversities of language, religion, customs, and institutions were tolerated. This was the achievement praised in the days of Rome's greatness by the Greek orator Aelius Aristides: "You have made the name of Rome no longer that of a city but of an entire people." It impressed the Christian poet Prudentius and his pagan and Christian contemporaries even in the period when Rome was in manifest decline: "A common law made them equals and bound them by a single name, bringing the conquered into bonds of brotherhood. We live in countries the most diverse like fellow-citizens of the same blood dwelling within the single ramparts of their native city and all united in an ancestral home." [1]

[1] Prudentius, *A Reply to Symmachus*, II, 608–612; tr. by H. J. Thomson, *Prudentius* (Loeb Classical Library; Cambridge, Mass., 1953), II, 55.

The Concept of a Universal Society

The ideal of a common citizenship in a unified world was cherished centuries after it had passed out of the realm of practical politics. Although a single Roman Empire was replaced by separate German kingdoms in the West and by an Eastern Roman Empire in Constantinople, men clung tenaciously to their belief in the eternity of the Roman Empire. Long after the living memory of Rome's centralized rule was lost, and when, in fact, the growth of feudalism made such rule impossible, the ideal continued to have an irresistible appeal. The coronation of Charlemagne as Holy Roman Emperor in 800 and of Otto the Great in 962 are concrete manifestations of the persistent conviction that the Roman Empire had never perished and that imperial might had not decayed but had been transferred to other monarchs. However slight may have been the actual strength of the Holy Roman Empire in its history of a thousand years, it was a witness to the evocative power of Rome's name. So, too, the mediaeval ideal of a *Respublica Christiana*, a commonwealth represented by the church, was essentially the Roman tradition of universality modified by Christian thought.

Roman Law

The Roman law, the instrument and the symbol of her unity, was Rome's greatest achievement. The acceptance of this legacy by the Middle Ages gave both church and state a basis for their own systems of law and helped to civilize Europe by spreading widely the principles of equity and humanity which were embodied in the structure of the law. Roman law did not share the fate of the Empire. The barbarian conquerors retained both Roman law and law courts for their Roman subjects, and for their fellow Germans they harmonized Roman law and legal concepts with their own law and customs. In the Eastern Roman Empire, Roman law and legal theory, as crystallized in Justinian's great codification, remained in force for almost a thousand years. In the East and West during the Middle Ages the church erected canon law, its own legal system, upon Roman foundations.

Thus Roman law remained a vital force in the centuries after the decline of the Empire. Then at the end of the eleventh century interest in its principles was rekindled by the study of Justinian's *Corpus Iuris Civilis* at Bologna in Italy, and before long the law became a major subject of study in the universities of Europe. By the sixteenth century Roman law was increasingly applied in the European courts of law, and it served as the basis for the legal systems of the states of continental Europe and their overseas colonies. It still performs its ancient mission of binding together disparate peoples, for a large part of the western world employs Roman law today. Even where legal systems, such as the common law of the English-speaking peoples, are not Roman in origin, many of their fundamental concepts are derived from Roman law and the very terms used to describe them are of Latin origin. Property, contract, agent, testament, judge, jury, crime: the terms and the legal and juridical concepts which they denominate are Roman.

Through its application Roman law has exercised a continuous influence upon the development of the law of the western world, but the underlying concepts of Roman law have equally influenced jurisprudence, philosophy, and politics. We have seen how from the time of Rome's earliest legal code, the Twelve Tables (c.443 B.C.), the harshness of the law was steadily modified. Under the impact first of Stoic philosophy and then of Christianity a greater emphasis was placed upon human rights and social justice, and the law became ever more enlightened. When the Roman jurists broadened their understanding of civil law to something like a "law of nations" and eventually to a kind of "natural law," they forged the link which binds Graeco-Roman and modern concepts of the rights and duties of the individual.

It is, however, not only in administration and law that the vitality of the Roman institutional heritage is apparent. The large estates or villas of the Later Empire, which were cultivated by half-free *coloni*, continued into the Middle Ages, and by a fusion of Roman and German elements became the manorial system of that period. Similarly the late Roman system of holding land under the protection of a strong landlord influenced feudal methods of land tenure in mediaeval Europe. Nor did the instruments by which Rome long maintained a flourishing urban life die. Even in the darkest period of the Middle Ages many Roman roads, although neglected, continued to be used. While Roman cities became impoverished and shrank in area and population, the more important ones never disappeared, but survived at least as centers of ecclesiastical administration and for such trade as existed. Today, fifteen hundred years after the end of the Western Empire, the traveler in Europe moves along the routes of ancient Roman roads and visits cities which have had a continuous history from antiquity to the present moment.

The Cultural Heritage

To Rome's practical skill as administrator and lawgiver we owe the preservation and dissemination of classical culture, for it was within the frame of institutions which they created that the Romans fashioned their culture by a synthesis of Greek, Oriental, and Roman elements. But for these institutions Roman culture and with it much of Greek culture might not have survived.

Rome's native culture had been changed as a result of her contacts with the Greeks of southern Italy and Sicily and eventually by her acquisition of the Greek East. The culture of her new subjects in the eastern provinces was Greek, and Roman culture itself was soon so thoroughly permeated with Hellenic elements that it may more accurately be described as Graeco-Roman. Roman schools began to offer a system of education which was essentially Greek. Greek literature, philosophy, and rhetoric were eagerly studied at Rome and became acknowledged models for Roman writers. Most of the literary forms employed by Roman authors, much of their imagery and symbolism, their mythology, the very meters of their poetry, were borrowed from the Greeks. Roman artists and architects adapted Greek canons and techniques of art and architecture to their own needs and made them an integral part of the Roman heritage to western civilization. By unifying and by Romanizing the ancient world the Romans enabled their culture, of which the Greek element was so important a part, to spread throughout the Mediterranean basin and western Europe. Strong enough to outlast the collapse of the Empire, Graeco-Roman civilization was preserved by the new states of western Europe, the Eastern Roman Empire, and the church.

Latin, the Language of Western Civilization

To the civilization which they developed the Romans contributed many distinctively Roman elements. Chief among these was the Latin language, which gradually replaced the native tongues of Rome's subjects in the western half of the Empire and which in time the German conquerors adopted as their own language of administration and literature. It was in Latin that the western church Fathers wrote; it was into Latin that St. Jerome translated the Bible; it was in Latin that for centuries poets, historians, and theologians wrote their works. The church in the West used Latin for its ritual and for its official documents, as it does even today. As the language of literature, learning, and law during the Middle Ages, Latin was in effect an international language which recognized no frontiers in the West. In contrast, therefore, to all the centrifugal forces of the period, Latin served as a bond of unity.

For a thousand years after the disintegration of the Empire, Latin survived as the leading, and for much of that time the only, language of literature. For learning and law it was supreme until the seventeenth and eighteenth centuries. Although Latin has been superseded by the modern languages for most scholarly and scientific purposes outside the church, it remains today an important part of the school curriculum wherever the European educational tradition prevails. Thus the key to the treasures of Latin literature has been handed down from generation to generation.

Even when Latin was no longer a regular means of communication, its influence remained strong. It was out of the popular or Vulgar Latin spoken by the common people of the Roman Empire that the Romance languages—Italian, French, Spanish, Portuguese, and Roumanian—gradually came into being during the Middle Ages. Moreover, such non-Latin languages as English contain a high proportion of words derived from Latin; in fact, it has been estimated that from half to two-thirds of the words commonly employed in English are of Latin origin. To Latin the English-speaking peoples owe a large part of their philosophic and scientific vocabulary as well as many of the words by which they denote political, social, and economic institutions. The very scripts used in mediaeval manuscripts were Roman in origin, and the Roman alphabet itself was adopted by the Romance, Celtic, and Germanic languages, several of the Slavic tongues, and by other languages such as Hungarian, Finnish, and Turkish. Clearly the Latin language is one of the greatest and most enduring of Rome's many bequests to western civilization.

For nearly two thousand years men have regarded Latin literature as a very precious part of their inheritance from ancient Rome. Despite their fears that they might be corrupted by them, the church Fathers of the early centuries read and studied Latin authors and by their own example showed how classical literature might be put to Christian uses. Even in the darkest period of the Middle Ages the ancient authors were not forgotten. In the monasteries, the centers of learning at that time, the monks copied and preserved the texts of classical authors, while in the newly established states of western Europe, Germanic kings were often active patrons of Latin letters. Throughout the Middle Ages the literature of ancient Rome remained a fundamental part of the course of study in the schools. When in the later Middle Ages the universities were founded, Latin literature was one of the staples of instruction. Either in its own right or by helping to shape the vernacular literature which eventually superseded it, Latin literature remained a vital force throughout the mediaeval period. With the Renaissance there came not a rebirth but an intensification of interest in a literature which had suffered vicissitudes but whose study had never been abandoned. Latin literature is read today by fewer people than in the past. It is, however, so firmly embedded in the western cultural tradition that it still wields a dominating influence. Scarcely a branch or genre of writing in the modern world can be named which has not to some extent been molded by the work of a Roman author. Cicero helped to fashion the language and thought of the western world, Seneca the philosophy and tragedy, Plautus and Terence the comedy, Virgil and Horace the poetry, Ovid the mythology.

The Roman legacy in architecture and art has been equally rich. Not only was Roman architecture a prime factor in the development of the ecclesiastical architecture of the Middle Ages, but it largely determined the plan of mediaeval secular buildings. The arch, the dome, and the vault—forms of construction which the Romans either developed out of their own creative genius or else made peculiarly their own—have had a continuous life in the East and the West from ancient times to our day. In painting, sculpture and the minor arts, too, Roman standards of craftsmanship and canons of taste have contributed immensely to the establishment of an artistic tradition in western civilization.

The Church as Heir of Rome

However great the Roman institutional and cultural heritage may be, it is overshadowed by one contribution which the Empire, by the very fact of its existence, made to western civilization. It was in the Roman Empire that Christianity came into being and finally won supremacy. The *Pax Romana*, the peace which Rome gave to the ancient world, facilitated the spread of Christianity and made possible the translation into reality of the ideal of a universal religion. When the political unity of the Roman world was destroyed, a new spiritual unity, represented by the church, took its place and served as a binding force for the Middle Ages.

In its triumph the church did not reject the past, but built upon Roman foundations and within the frame furnished by the Roman Empire. From Rome the church inherited its institutions, its organization, its administrative system, and its law. From Rome the church in the West received the Latin language, a potent instrument of unity. Latin literature and learning gave a higher intellectual quality to Christianity, and Roman art furnished the basic forms for Christian art. By accepting and making its own this rich Roman heritage, the church built a bridge between the ancient world and the modern.

Western civilization rests upon Greek, Roman, and Hebrew-Christian foundations. To Rome we owe an incalculable debt for building a great civilization in which was incorporated and preserved the Graeco-Oriental culture which she herself inherited and for providing a setting into which Christianity, her own heir, could come into being. For more than two thousand years the western world has been taught and inspired by Rome. Deeply rooted in western civilization, Roman ideals and practices still bear witness to the magnificent achievement of Eternal Rome.

Epilogue

THE four centuries from the accession of Marcus Aurelius to the death of Justinian saw the decline of the Roman Empire and the development of mediaeval Europe. During those centuries the Roman peace was broken and the Empire split asunder. In the East, Roman emperors were strong enough to maintain an Eastern Roman or Byzantine Empire for a thousand years, but upon the ruins of the western half of the old Roman Empire the Germanic peoples built their kingdoms. In East and West during these centuries Christianity triumphed over the pagan gods and became the dominant religion. Far-reaching changes in government, society, economy, and culture were both cause and result of this transformation of form and spirit which signified the decline of the ancient world and the emergence of the mediaeval world.

Between the two phases of history there was no abrupt break. Roman civilization, which incorporated the great contributions of Greece and the Orient, was the cement which bound the ancient period to the mediaeval and gave a unity and a continuity to the course of European history. Battered though it was by the storms which marked the decline of the Empire, Roman civilization survived and received fresh strength from its union with Christianity. "Eternal Rome" is more than a familiar phrase which describes the ancient capital of the Empire; it expresses the immortality of the precious heritage of Roman civilization. "Its importance in universal history it can never lose," the great historian Lord Bryce said. "For into it all the life of the ancient world was gathered, out of it all the life of the modern world arose."

Chronological Summary

Establishment of Gallic empire by Postumus.
Revolt of Palmyra under Queen Zenobia.
Germanic invasions.

268–270   Claudius Gothicus.
Defeat of the Goths.

270–275   Aurelian.
Evacuation of the province of Dacia.

284–305   Diocletian.

301   Edict of Diocletian.

302–304   Persecution of the Christians.

4th and   Ammianus Marcellinus—Roman historian; Claudian
early   and Ausonius—Latin poets; Donatus—grammarian;
5th   Arnobius and Lactantius—Latin Christian theolo-
centuries gians; Prudentius—Latin Christian poet; Eusebius—
           church historian; Gregory of Nyssa and Gregory
           of Nazianzus—Greek theologians; Basil—monastic
           rules for the East; Ambrose, Jerome, Augustine—
           Latin Church Fathers.

306–337   Constantine.

313   Edict of Milan.

325   Council of Nicaea.

330   Founding of Constantinople.

c.340   Conversion of Goths to Christianity by Wulfila.

353–361   Constantius.

361–363   Julian the Apostate.

364–378   Valens.

c.370   Appearance of Huns in Europe.

378   Battle of Adrianople.
Beginning of barbarian invasions.

378–395   Theodosius I.

381   Primacy of bishops of Rome recognized by Council
          of Constantinople.

395   Permanent division of Roman Empire into eastern and
          western empires.

5th century	Rutilius Namatianus and Sidonius Apollinaris—Latin poets; Benedict—Benedictine Rule for western monasticism.
c.400	Withdrawal of Romans from Britain.
408–450	Theodosius II.
410	Sack of Rome by Visigoths under Alaric.
c.418	Establishment of Visigothic kingdom in Gaul.
429	Establishment of Vandal kingdom in Africa.
438	Theodosian Code.
440–461	Pope Leo I.
c.450	Anglo-Saxon settlement in Britain. Establishment of Burgundian kingdom in Gaul.
451	Defeat of Attila and the Huns at Campus Mauriacus.
455	Sack of Rome by Vandals.
c.460	Establishment of Visigothic kingdom in Spain. Establishment of Frankish kingdom in Gaul.
475–476	Romulus Augustulus.
476	End of Western Roman Empire.
486–511	Clovis, king of the Franks.
488	Establishment of Ostrogothic kingdom in Italy.
492–496	Pope Gelasius I.
493–526	Theodoric, king of the Ostrogoths. Boethius—philosopher, and Cassiodorus—Christian writer.
6th and early 7th centuries	Gregory of Tours—historian of Frankish Gaul; Fortunatus—poet in Gaul; Isidore of Seville—encyclopedist in Visigothic Spain.
527–565	Justinian.
527–548	Theodora, empress. Procopius—historian.
529–534	Publication of *Corpus Iuris Civilis.*
532	Nika Riots.
532–537	Construction of St. Sophia in Constantinople.
533	Recovery of Africa.

535–555 Recovery of Italy and southern Spain.
c.540 Monophysite heresy.
568 Invasion of Italy by Lombards.
590–604 Pope Gregory the Great.

Suggestions for Further Reading

THE reader has a choice among several good one-volume histories of Rome: A. E. R. Boak, *History of Rome to 565 A.D.* (3d ed.; New York, 1952); M. Cary, *History of Rome* (London, 1935); A. A. Trever, *History of Ancient Civilization*, Vol. II, *The Roman World* (New York, 1939). R. H. Barrow, *The Romans* (Pelican Books, 1949), is a brief and sympathetic account of the Roman character and achievement.

For the Empire one book, a masterpiece of literature and history, towers above all others although it is antiquated in detail and extravagant in its judgments: Edward Gibbon, *The History of the Decline and Fall of the Roman Empire* (originally published in London, 1776–1788; best ed. by J. B. Bury, London, 1909–1914, 7 vols.). Gibbon's account to the end of the fifth century has been skillfully abridged by Dero A. Saunders, *The Portable Gibbon* (New York, 1952). M. P. Charlesworth, *The Roman Empire* (London, 1951), is an admirable brief account of the first three centuries; the *Cambridge Ancient History*, Vol. XII (Cambridge, 1939), examines in detail the latter half of the period to the death of Constantine and furnishes full bibliographies; illustrations for the period are in *Cambridge Ancient History*, Vol. of Plates V (Cambridge, 1939).

Various aspects of imperial history are treated by *Oxford Classical Dictionary* (Oxford, 1949), which has articles and brief bibliographies on separate topics; Theodor Mommsen, *The*

Provinces of the Roman Empire (2d ed.; New York, 1909, 2 vols.), a classic of historical scholarship, which should be supplemented by M. I. Rostovtzeff's magisterial and challenging *Social and Economic History of the Roman Empire* (Oxford, 1926) and by more specialized studies: Samuel Dill, *Roman Society in the Last Century of the Western Empire* (2d ed.; London, 1899); T. R. Glover, *Life and Literature in the Fourth Century* (Cambridge, 1901). C. G. Starr, *Civilization and the Caesars: The Intellectual Revolution in the Roman Empire* (Ithaca, N.Y., 1954), is a penetrating evaluation of the impact of intellectual changes upon the Roman Empire. F. W. Walbank, *The Decline of the Roman Empire in the West* (London, 1946), is a thoughtful analysis of the central problem of the causes of decline.

Of the vast literature on the oriental religions in the Roman Empire and especially on Christianity only a few titles can be indicated. The New Testament, of course, is the basic source for the history of the rise of Christianity. C. H. Cochrane, *Christianity and Classical Culture* (2d ed.; London, 1944); Franz Cumont, *Oriental Religions in Roman Paganism* (London, 1911), and *The Mysteries of Mithra* (2d ed.; Chicago, 1911); E. R. Goodenough, *The Church in the Roman Empire* (New York, 1931); A. H. M. Jones, *Constantine and the Conversion of Europe* (London, 1949); P. C. de Labriolle, *History and Literature of Christianity* (New York, 1924); M. L. W. Laistner, *Christianity and Pagan Culture in the Later Roman Empire* (Ithaca, N.Y., 1951); A. D. Nock, *Conversion. The Old and the New in Religion* (Oxford, 1933).

There is no dearth of books on the age of transition: the *Cambridge Medieval History*, Vol. I (2d ed., Cambridge, 1936) and Vol. II (Cambridge, 1936), which gives a detailed account by specialists who have provided full bibliographies; C. W. Previté-Orton, *The Shorter Cambridge Medieval History*, Vol. I (Cambridge, 1952), is an abridgement; R. F. Arragon, *The Transition from the Ancient to the Medieval World* (New York, 1936); J. B. Bury, *History of the Later Roman Empire, 395–565* (2 vols.; London, 1923) and *The Invasion of Europe by the Barbarians* (London, 1928); Ferdinand Lot, *The End of the Ancient World and the Beginnings of the Middle Ages* (New York, 1931); H. St. L. B. Moss, *The Birth of the Middle Ages, 395–814* (2d ed.; London, 1947); E. K. Rand, *Founders of the Middle Ages* (2d ed.; Cambridge, Mass., 1929); F. A. Wright, *A History of Later Greek Literature* (London, 1932); F. A. Wright and T. A. Sinclair, *A History of Later Latin Literature* (London, 1931).

Justinian's reign and the Eastern Roman Empire may be studied in: N. H. Baynes, *The Byzantine Empire* (2d ed.; Oxford, 1943); N. H. Baynes and H. St. L. B. Moss, *Byzantium* (Oxford, 1948); and P. N. Ure, *Justinian and His Age* (Pelican Books, 1951).

The Roman institutional and cultural heritage is discussed by several authors in Cyril Bailey, *The Legacy of Rome* (Oxford, 1923). Gilbert Highet, *The Classical Tradition* (Oxford, 1949), describes the Greek and Roman influences on western literature.

Although the writers of the period may not measure up to the standards of classical literature, they give a more vivid picture of thought and action during the late Empire than any modern work. The historian Ammianus Marcellinus on the fourth century, and Procopius on Justinian, Marcus Aurelius' *Meditations*, the pagan and Christian poets, and St. Augustine's great works, *Confessions* and *The City of God*, are available in translations in the Loeb Classical Library or Everyman's Library. Finally, even a random sampling of the laws will give the reader a sense of the mounting crisis in the Empire. Clyde Pharr, *The Theodosian Code* (Princeton, 1952), provides a translation of this fascinating source.

Index